ONLINE TEACHING WITH ZOOM

A GUIDE FOR TEACHING AND LEARNING WITH VIDEOCONFERENCE PLATFORMS

AARON JOHNSON

Trademarks: Zoom is the trademark of Zoom, https://zoom.us

First Paperback Edition July 2020

ISBN 978-0-9897116-3-0 (paperback)

ISBN 978-0-9897116-4-7 (ebook)

https://excellentonlineteaching.com

To Monte—

You've modeled the heart of this book

for your students and colleagues.

CONTENTS

PART V

WRAPPING UP

INTRODUCTION

My grandfather was part of the Greatest Generation, who weathered the Great Depression and enlisted to fight in World War 2. He once told me that learning a particular technology changed the course of his life. As a teenager, he decided to sit down at a typewriter. Investing hours in developing the skill of typing, he became quite fast at the keyboard. When the Coast Guard learned of this ability, they sent him alone by train, then by boat, to a remote and secret radar station in Newfoundland, Canada, where he coded and decoded messages about the locations of enemy ships and submarines in the Atlantic.

After the war, his skills led him to study journalism, get his degree, then begin work at a newspaper. He watched homes fitted for indoor plumbing, and radio move to television. He went from using the telegraph in the service to using the telephone to conduct business. In his decades as a reporter, then editor, my grandfather transitioned from a manual typewriter to a series of electric versions, then to an early computer, and later to a personal computer. In his nineties, he purchased and began using an iPad.

I admire his approach to technology because he considered each new invention as a tool. From working on farms and in the family iron foundry, he knew that tools required time and focused attention. Tools entailed practice. He brought that mindset to the typewriter and to the digital tools he would later adopt.

Videoconferencing software, like **Zoom, is a tool.**[1] Cal Newport, Professor of Computer Science at Georgetown University, has explained that digital tools, like Zoom, are so effortless to pick up and use that we easily forget that they are complex tools and require this same intentional use and practice.[2] I've designed this book to help you acquire and practice the skills to use this tool for the specific purpose of education.

Transitioning from an on-campus classroom to an on-Zoom classroom can generate some serious anxiety. We don't want to screw it up or look incompetent. We want to function with confidence and for our students to get the best possible experience. As you read this book, I hope that it helps you to gain competency and confidence as a video-conferencing educator. If you've been teaching with videoconference software for a while, this guide will help you sharpen your skills.

The Essential Idea and Its Implications

As futurists and philosophers like Kevin Kelley and Marshal McLuhan remind us, every technology comes with latent strengths and weak-nesses. And like every tool, Zoom has certain tendencies. The essential idea of this book is that **Zoom was built for conversations.** It was designed for dialogue and discourse. This essential idea has two major implications.

First, **we must cultivate an active learning environment.** To use video-conferencing for 100% lecture is like using a butter knife to tighten a screw. It kind of works, but we are forcing the tool and go against the grain of its design. Based on this essential idea, *Online Teaching with Zoom* will help you create and support an active learning remote class-room. The good news is that this does not require you to reinvent your lessons. Instead, we'll look at ways to adapt your material and lead your learners in this unique space.

Second, **we must learn how to set up and facilitate Zoom Breakout groups**. Breakout groups are the most important and powerful educational tool in our Zoom toolbox. They allow us to split our larger classroom into smaller learning teams. However, learning groups don't work out-of-the-box. Teaching and learning in breakout groups requires understanding group dynamics, some preparation, and skill in facilitating learning teams. *Part 4: Working with Breakout Groups* is a guide to building spaces where learners can thrive in collaborative and discussion-driven learning experiences.

Online Teaching

Videoconferencing opens the door to a variety of blended and hybrid formats, different ways of combining asynchronous and synchronous delivery. It's beyond the scope of *Online Teaching with Zoom* to explore these in detail. Instead, these pages focus on a very specific form of online teaching: the synchronous video experience. Still, you will find the principles, practices, and tips in this book transferrable to any online format where you use videoconferencing as a teaching tool.

How to Use this Book

I've written this book in the trenches alongside teachers and students. Its pages are a response to their questions about how to teach and learn in this new virtual space. Educators have an incredible volume of work, and we are always short on time. That's why this book will skip the history and development of videoconferencing. It's not our purpose to discuss telecommunication theories. *Online Teaching with Zoom* is more of a guidebook you can consult to get started in the videoconferenced classroom and a quick-reference manual for structuring your class sessions and facilitating interaction in the Zoom classroom.

Part 1: The Technical Stuff is designed to help you become proficient with Zoom and its features. It's not a detailed technical manual, but a higher-level guide intended to address the essential elements. Our goal is to get the technology out of the way so that we can focus on teaching and learning. If you're looking for a more detailed set of technical instructions, you can find the best resource at Zoom's Support site.[3] Because software is continuously updated, I've attempted to focus only on those technical elements that are more enduring.

Part 2: A Recipe for Success roots our teaching in the student experience. It asks, "How do students experience the videoconferenced classroom?" and "Being aware of this, how can educators create a classroom environment most conducive for learning?" The second chapter in this segment details a set of classroom protocols. These will help your learners get their learning space squared away and come to class ready to contribute to the learning community.

Part 3: Active Learning in Zoom provides thirty different active learning methods, a list of key practices for adapting your instruction, and ten practices for facilitating learning in an active learning experience.

Part 4: Working with Breakout Groups explores how to create effective learning teams. These chapters will help you set up groups, set expectations, and develop Zoom Preps and discussion guides. Part 4 concludes with a chapter to help you develop the critical skills for facilitating learning in Zoom breakouts and large group discussions.

Part 5: Improving our Game contains a final chapter on how we can leverage the tools in Zoom to create opportunities for student feedback, then use that feedback to improve our teaching.

The Companion Website: Software is regularly updated. Because screenshots and images in this book would quickly become outdated, I've instead created a website to host the visual elements, like screenshots and tutorials. This companion website also includes downloadable resources and links to many of the book's referenced materials. (In an effort to make the book available before the Fall 2020 term, the book will be published before the website is complete). The site is organized by chapters so that you can quickly find the information. You can access the site at **https://excellentonlineteaching.com/online-teaching-with-zoom-resources**

Bonus Material: Finally, I have a gift for you: **5 Bonus Chapters** that you can download from the *Online Teaching with Zoom* companion site. These are like a cookbook, containing one chapter on how to structure Zoom sessions and four chapters of teaching and learning templates. You can access the bonus material at **https://excellentonlineteaching. com/otwz-bonus**

Let's start teaching with Zoom!

1 THE TECHNICAL STUFF

- The Equipment
- Prepare Your Classroom
- Testing and Technical Difficulties
- Sharing
- Breakout Room Basics
- Chat
- Polls
- Security

GOAL: to become proficient with Zoom so that we can move from hesitant to confident, and create a warm, secure, and hospitable environment for learning.

Part I

The Technical Stuff

1

THE EQUIPMENT

> No matter how long you have been using a tool, endless upgrades make you into a newbie—the new user often seen as clueless. In this era of 'becoming', everyone becomes a newbie. Worse, we will be newbies forever. That should keep us humble."
>
> — Kevin Kelly, *The Inevitable: Understanding the 12 Technological Forces That Will Shape Our Future*

OUR GOAL in Part 1 is to become teachers who are proficient with our tools so that we can focus on our teaching and our students' learning. We experience anxiety when learning a new technology, especially when we have twenty, tuition-paying, digital native students watching us. We are not aiming for mastery. However, that will come with time and practice. Right now, we want to set a strong technical foundation. We'll start by looking at the equipment you need to create a warm and inviting learning experience.

Most teachers are not enamored with technology. For some of us, it's a necessary evil. We love teaching. And we don't want to get diverted by fixing technical issues or sidetracked by non-essential software features. In short, we want to get the tech out of the way so that our students can have the best possible experience. This chapter helps you to do just that. We'll look at the essential pieces of equipment you'll need and review a few details on how to set things up so that you can deliver an uninterrupted and quality experience to your students. You'll find updated links to some of the equipment mentioned in this chapter at the *Online Teaching with Zoom website*. [1]

First, Audio is Everything

You can lose your video signal and still communicate. Lose your audio, and the session is over. Because of this, we need to start by prioritizing audio. Mediocre audio quality is tolerable in short meetings, but first-rate audio becomes vital for longer and regular teaching sessions. The more energy our learners must exert to hear and understand what we are saying, the less energy they have at their disposal for the hard work of learning. Because only our students hear our voice, we can easily overlook audio quality. This is why it's so important to test our audio by recording and listening to a short segment.

Most devices come with an adequate microphone built into them. However, we won't know our sound quality until we test it. To check, log in to your videoconferencing software and play with the audio settings. In Zoom, you can access a test meeting room at https://zoom.us/test. In the audio settings, you can record a small segment and replay your audio. Record your voice and replay it a few times, giving attention to the volume, the way sound bounces off the walls of your space, and ambient noise or buzzing. Does your voice sound full and pleasant? Or does the microphone limit the range of your voice and make it feel distant or anemic? If you plan to teach this way often, you will want to purchase a quality microphone, one that picks up the full range of your voice, so that your audio is warm and full, giving your students a more pleasant experience. (I'll publish a list of several USB and Bluetooth microphones at the *Online Teaching with Zoom webpage* for this chapter).

With a desktop microphone, the volume and tonal change as we move around. It's important to place our microphone close to us and to keep it at the same distance from our mouth throughout the session. Closer proximity to the mic allows it to pick up the full range of our voice and gives our students a consistent experience.

Headsets and earbuds help to localize sound. Because earbud and headset microphones stay at a fixed distance from our mouth, the audio volume and quality remain the same. The drawback of a headset is that it makes you look like an air traffic controller. It may not seem like a big deal, but a headset puts the tech visually out front, and it's our goal to move the tech into the background.

Bluetooth earbuds are less conspicuous, and their noise-canceling features make a notable difference by eliminating background noise. Apple and Bose both make more expensive, high-quality Bluetooth earbuds, but there are some reliable and less-expensive options available. However, I've noticed that most Bluetooth earbuds, including Apple's AirPods Pro, can make the speaker sound like they are talking into a tin can. I've observed that most wired earbuds provide superior audio to the Bluetooth versions. At the end of the day, I prefer not to be tethered. For that reason, I use a desktop USB microphone. (See the companion webpage for this chapter where I test a variety of microphones).

After plugging in a USB microphone or connecting a Bluetooth device, you'll need to select it within audio settings. In the bottom left-hand corner of the Zoom window, you'll see a microphone icon. There is an up-arrow just to the right of the icon. Click on this to reveal the audio menu. Next, select the correct microphone from the list.

Your Backup Microphone

"Two is one, and one is none." That quote is from one of my broad-casting professors in college. It means you always need to think through your backup equipment. When for no discernible reason, your microphone isn't working, what will you use as your backup? Know how to switch back over to your built-in computer audio quickly. The key is being ready. Invest a few minutes getting used to the audio controls in Zoom, or your other videoconferencing software, by practicing the switch between different audio devices.

Your Camera

You will need an HD camera that you can position at eye level. Most of the time, a built-in laptop or desktop camera will suffice. From testing several external HD webcams, I've found that Logitech makes the best quality and most reliable product. They rest on the top of a monitor, and you can adjust them for the best angle. Most of these webcams contain built-in microphones, but the audio is usually mediocre. Because of this, I still recommend using one of the audio solutions recommended above.

Your camera's angle is a critical element, and its importance is too often overlooked. The camera angle and your posture will communicate an ongoing and tacit message to your students. Filmmakers will tell you that camera angles are their go-to tool for conveying their message, especially power dynamics—and power dynamics impact learning. Here is a quick overview of what different camera angles communicate:

- Camera positioned below eye-level: We are looking down onto our learners and inadvertently expressing dominance. It is also less than flattering because the shot features our neck and highlights our nostrils.
- Camera positioned above eye-level: We are looking up to our students. If you're short like me, perhaps you're accustomed to this. On camera, this can inadvertently communicate passivity and a lack of authority.
- Camera positioned from the side or at an irregular angle: This communicates that things are off-kilter, disorganized, or that we are inattentive and unaware.

- Camera positioned at eye-level: This communicates we are all on a level playing field and that things are stable.

Laptops require some creativity to get at eye-level. The best solution is an adjustable standing desk, the kind you can place on top of an existing workspace. Not only does this help us set the right camera angle, but it also allows us to alternate between sitting and standing. If you need a temporary solution, find a box or use a stack of books to raise your laptop to eye-level.

Once I've positioned my camera, I often need to adjust my chair height. It's easy to forget this low-tech feature built into most office chairs. It's a quick and easy way to get at eye-level with your camera and students.

If you are using a phone or tablet, you'll need a way to keep your device stationary and stable. I don't recommend using mobile devices for videoconference teaching because they have some software limitations. They reduce screen size, and I find it more challenging to share presentations and documents with them. However, if this is your only or primary device, acquire an adjustable device holder that you can attach to your desk.

Your Monitor

For many of us, our main computer is a laptop, so we sacrifice screen size for portability. The more I teach with Zoom, the more I'm convinced that an external monitor is a necessity. Monitor size becomes even more important when we have larger classes and need to accommodate more students on the screen. If, like me, you wear glasses, or just experience eye strain at work, then seriously consider acquiring a larger external monitor to care for your eyes. Additionally, with an external monitor, you can take advantage of the dual-screen features built into Zoom, like putting your presentation on one screen and your students on the second screen.

For both benefit and cost, I've found that a 32-inch monitor is optimal for videoconferencing. The key feature you want to look for is that it has the *correct input for your computer*. For most of us, that's going to be an HDMI cable input. In addition to the monitor, you'll need the correct type of HDMI cable that will connect with your computer's output. (See this chapter's companion webpage for links to monitors).

Student Equipment

Your course syllabus or classroom protocols should state that participation in the course requires a webcam, microphone, and reliable internet connection. Communicate this in a prominent place on your course site and your syllabus and repeat it in your course messaging. Beyond this, we have little control over what devices students may use to access our class. Some will use phones, and others will use laptops or tablets. The most important thing is that they know *how* to access your Zoom classroom with their particular device and to test it *before* class. If you can recommend one piece of equipment to your students that will make the most difference for everyone's experience, it is to ask them all to wear headsets or earbuds. These cut out ambient noise and make it possible to have an unmuted classroom, something I'll recommend in future chapters. If students have no other choice but to access the virtual classroom using public WiFi, then headsets or earbuds are a necessity.

Besides these basic tech requirements, I share with my students some technical responsibilities and protocols for the course. We'll address at those in a later chapter on *Classroom Protocols*, and I'll provide you with an editable protocol document at the *Online Teaching with Zoom* website.[2]

I want to end this chapter with an important statement: *Good Enough is Good Enough*. I don't want you to read this and feel like you have to go out and drop $500 on equipment. Start with what you have and add to your toolbox in increments. See what you can borrow from your school or friends. Test things out to see what works best for you.

2

PREPARE YOUR CLASSROOM

 Man must shape his tools, lest they shape him."

— Arthur Miller

ALL OF US need a cheat sheet when we are trying out something new. Think of this chapter as your cheat sheet or pre-flight checklist before stepping into your Zoom classroom. I work at a graduate school, and our instructors like to arrive at least twenty minutes early to class. They set up their equipment, make sure there are no technical issues, arrange furniture, and get any other logistical stuff out of the way. That's what we are doing here. Work through this list, and you'll be ready and feel prepared to teach in this new space.

#1 Get in there and Play

Click into your Zoom room and spend time getting oriented. Become acquainted with all of the features. Don't worry; you're the only person in the room and you can't break anything. Just like a sports practice, work through some drills. Here's a sample list of some of the things you can work through:

- Run through all your audio and video settings. As mentioned in the previous chapter, switch back and forth between your audio devices.
- Open your Participants list and click through all the buttons, including the *mute all,* and *unmute all* buttons. You can turn on and off an individual participant's audio as well, but you will need a colleague to join you in the meeting to test this feature.
- Zoom has keyboard shortcuts for muting and unmuting as well as for many of its other functions. Review these at their website and practice using the shortcuts you expect will come in handy.[1]
- Click into Chat and send a message to everyone.
- *Share a file* via Chat. (This requires that you have file sharing enabled in your Zoom settings).[2]
- Mute/Unmute your audio in the bottom control bar.
- Try out the different reactions (also in the bottom control bar).
- Click on *Record* button. Pause the recording, resume it, then stop the recording.
- Stop your video, then restart it. Learning to start and stop video quickly becomes important for when you take breaks.
- Click on the *Poll* button and create a quick question.
- Click on *Share* to screen share a presentation, a document, your desktop, and the whiteboard. Switch back to your camera by clicking on *Stop Share.*
- Share another document, then click *Stop Share.* Going back and forth from *Share* to the main screen will likely be the thing you do most often.
- Ask a couple of colleagues or friends to join you in practicing Breakout Rooms. Create two breakouts, rename them, explore the options menu in the breakouts, exit breakouts. Do this several times, and take turns being in the student role so that you can get a feel for what it's like to be a participant.

If you've not taught a class with Zoom before, this will probably be the best 20-30 minutes you will invest. The familiarity you gain will replace fear and apprehension with a sense of confidence in this new space.

I'm going to get a bit psychological for a moment. From my experiences teaching amazing and squirrelly high school students, I learned to think of my classroom as "my territory." When you step into my room, I own the space, and I set the tone and culture in that space. I think it's helpful to have this same mindset with my Zoom classroom. Students desire a strong, clear, and more directive leadership style from their instructors when they enter a new and disorienting space like this. Your competence with the technical basics of the Zoom classroom is the foundation for your sense of ownership. Your students will sense this within the first few minutes of class.

#2 Lighting Essentials

Eliminate any bright light sources behind you and place a soft, diffused light source in front of you. A bright light source behind you will constrict the aperture on your camera and darken your image, sometimes making it impossible to see your facial features. Two of my siblings have hearing impairments. It's essential to have a clear view of a person's lips to discern what they are saying. Because of this, good lighting is also an issue of accessibility for many students.

If you can't avoid a rear light source, like a window, close the blinds or curtains to diffuse and reduce its intensity. Overhead lighting or a lamp in the background can blast students with light and cause similar problems. Turn them off or reposition your camera so that these light sources are not within your screen. However, you may encounter the opposite problem and not have enough light. To your students, you end up looking like Emperor Palpatine from Star Wars. The most straightforward solution is to sit in front of a window and adjust the blinds to get the right amount of light. If that's not possible, consider purchasing an inexpensive ring lamp with adjustable light levels and tones.

#3 Eye Contact and Appearance

Make eye contact with your students by looking directly into the camera or at least near your camera. Looking directly into the camera can feel strange at first and easy to forget. A helpful trick is to draw a smiley face or get a smiley face sticker and stick it on your computer next to the camera. It's silly, but it works.

Take a few moments to observe yourself in the camera preview. Most of us want to avoid looking at ourselves, but we need to be aware of how we appear to our students. One student shared with me, "It drives me crazy how many of my teachers have their laptops set up like this —with their cameras cutting off part of their face or looking up their nose." Light and medium tone shirts tend to play better on camera than dark shirts. Avoid striped and patterned shirts (like herringbone) as these can create a moiré pattern that can be incredibly distracting. A moiré pattern is an optical phenomenon where the patterns in clothing appear to jitter, swim, or shift. This makes it hard for our viewers' eyes to focus and creates unnecessary cognitive demand.

Make sure your camera is stable. I once observed an instructor teaching from a laptop on his lap while rocking in a rocking chair. I think we all got seasick during that session. Even though it's called a laptop, don't place your computer on your lap. This creates too much camera movement and amplifies the I'm-looking-down-on-you angle.

#4 Avoid Teaching in Public Spaces

Avoid using public wireless for Zoom sessions—unless that is your only option. Busy settings like airports, coffee shops, or co-working spaces may be okay for a one-on-one conversation with a student or a quick meeting. We grow accustomed to this, but such areas with ambient noise and movement distract our students. In other words, just because it's possible doesn't mean it's a good idea. The number of users on a public network will limit your bandwidth and may impair your connection. Teaching outdoors presents similar issues. Wind noise, barking dogs, nearby traffic, can all interfere with our audio.

Additionally, being outdoors often puts us outside the optimal range of our wireless router, resulting in connection problems.

#5 Test Your Connection and Your Internet Bandwidth

If teaching from home, you may need to make sure family members are not streaming movies or playing online video games during Zoom sessions. However, much will depend on the bandwidth provided by your internet service provider. If you are teaching from a work setting, you'll want to test your connection before the session to ensure a company firewall will not block your access. (See the companion webpage for this chapter for resources to test your internet bandwidth and review Zoom's bandwidth requirements).[3]

#6 Arrive Early

Just as you arrive early to prepare for your on-campus classroom, plan to sign in early to your online Zoom classroom. Use this time to prepare and open any documents for screen sharing, test your equipment, and converse with students who come to class early. Compared to most classrooms, the Zoom classroom is technically complicated. By getting in early, you simplify things, creating margin for yourself and space to connect with your students.

#7 Send A Reminder

Before your first session, email your students to remind them to test their equipment before the meeting. Provide your students with the Zoom Test Room link in your course site and your messaging.[4] I've provided an email template on the *Online Teaching with Zoom website* you can copy, customize, and send to your students.[5]

#8 Be Ready for the Worst

Know how to mute your students' microphones and how to shut down their video stream. Think of this as knowing where to get the fire extin-

guisher in case there is a fire. Like extinguishing fires, muting participants should not become a regular practice. However, we need to
know how to shut things down quickly when encountering the rare
circumstance of a student and spouse argument or a student who has
thought they turned off their camera and is changing their clothes.

#9 Provide a Single Entrance to Your Classroom

Provide your students with one link to your online Zoom meeting that
they can revisit for every meeting in their semester, quarter, etc. Scheduling multiple meetings takes unnecessary work and creates confu-
sion. The exact definition of Murphy's Law applies here: if you give
people more than one way to do something, they are more likely to
choose the wrong way. For instance, one teacher I know set up unique
meetings in different weeks of her course site. During week four, she
accidentally went into the week-three meeting room. She was in there
for a long time, wondering why none of her students were showing up
for class.

Zoom now has a scheduling feature built into their LMS integrations.
(LMS stands for Learning Management System, such software as
Moodle, Blackboard, Canvas, etc.) These integrations are great because
they provide another layer of security. Students must first log in to the
LMS the Zoom meeting link. It simplifies things by generating a single
module within the course site for your students to access the class
meetings. Additionally, the LMS integration will create an archive of
any recorded class sessions and organize them by date. (LMS Integrations are only available for institutions with an upgraded account).

Now that you have the basics down and your classroom set up, let's
address how to handle technical difficulties.

3

TESTING AND TECHNICAL DIFFICULTIES

 A computer once beat me at chess, but it was no match for me at kickboxing."

— Emo Philips

"IT JUST WORKS" is the tagline Zoom users bestowed on the software. I've found this to be accurate, especially when comparing Zoom with other video conferencing solutions. The others required Adobe Flash and Java updates that got in the way by causing technical interruptions. Regardless of the video conferencing software you choose, there will always be the weakest link in the chain, something beyond your control. The weakest links are typically the equipment used by individual students and their internet connection. And the more students you have in your Zoom classroom, the more likely you are to run into technical difficulties. Technical interruptions should be the exception, but we all need a plan for when these occur.

Head It Off at the Pass

First, the good news: Most of these issues can be identified and corrected *before* your class session by requiring your students to test their equipment. As mentioned in the previous chapter, direct them to the Zoom Test Room link or an equivalent URL for your video conferencing software.[1] Here your students can click into and adjust their audio and video settings. By selecting the correct camera and mic on their device, they will get a visual and audio preview to verify their audio and video are working. Now that they are also familiar with the interface, they can go in and make changes quickly.

During testing, we've had students encounter the *Red Screen Issue*. Instead of seeing their video, students see a red screen, or perhaps just black. On newer devices, this is caused by a plastic privacy shield that they can slide over their camera lens. The solution is so easy that it's humorous: slide or lift the shield away from the camera. This problem typically happens to students who are not yet familiar with their new devices.

A similar and more common issue comes into play with microphones that have an on/off switch. Again, the solutions are easy to overlook. They are as simple as turning the microphone switch to the *ON* position, or going into the computer software and unmuting the computer microphone.

On occasion, a student will experience significant or recurring technical issues. Here's my rule of thumb: *unless it's something you can solve in 15 seconds, don't try to resolve your students' technical problems.* Instead, create an *If You Have Technical Difficulties* section in your course site or syllabus. You can download an editable template for this at the *Online Teaching with Zoom* site.[2] These instructions direct the student first to leave the session and rejoin. Often this reconnects video and audio devices and fixes the problem. If that doesn't resolve the issue, have them reach out to a classmate who may be willing to help or ask them to contact your institution's technical Help Desk. If they can receive audio, they can continue to listen, and they can participate by typing into the chat window, then work with tech support to figure things out after class. If it's a poor connection issue, then it can only be remedied by students improving their WiFi connection by getting closer to the router, hardwiring their computer using an ethernet cable, or by contacting their internet service provider. When all else fails, students can connect using Zoom's join meeting by phone option.[3]

Because student-side technical issues can be difficult and time-consuming to diagnose, you want students first to know that they are responsible for finding the solutions. Second, you want to direct them to the professionals at your institution who have the time and expertise to serve them. Referring students to the experts doesn't mean you are hanging them out to dry. You are directing them to the best steps and best resources—during the middle of teaching a class, this is not going to be you.

Your Backup Plan

What if *your* equipment or connection fails? This is the situation you want to rehearse and perhaps type out. As with student technical difficulties, don't spend much time troubleshooting. Instead, be decisive and promptly communicate your plan to your students. Here are a few scenarios and how I recommend we respond:

- If you have a very poor internet connection and cannot proceed with class: open Chat and tell your students you will have to end the session. Before closing the meeting, wait for students to read your message and to chat back with any questions. Let them know you'll be on Chat for another 5 minutes to take questions. Follow up immediately with an email to the group to instruct them on how you will reschedule the session or other means of accomplishing the work.
- If your connection is good, but you have no audio or video: bring up the Chat window and communicate that you are going to close out the session and return to see if that will fix the problem. If that doesn't fix the problem, proceed the same way as the first scenario.
- If you have audio, but can't get the video to work, and you've

already left and rejoined the meeting without the problem resolving: inform your students that you'll be participating via audio-only and continue with the class.

With that out of the way, we are now going to move into chapters on specific teaching tools and how to use them effectively: Sharing, Chat, Breakouts, and Polls.

4

SHARING

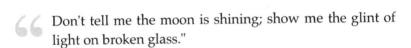 Don't tell me the moon is shining; show me the glint of light on broken glass."

— Anton Chekhov

Does This Sound Familiar?

"WHERE IS THAT STUPID GRAPH?" She said this under her breath, low enough so that none of her students could hear. But they did hear because her microphone amplified her muttering. Adrian began searching through her computer files. "What did I name that thing?" Looking past her file manager window, she could see fourteen pairs of eyes on the screen staring back at her and waiting. "Okay, well, I can't seem to find it, so how about we skip that, and we'll pick up there next week. In the fifteen minutes we have left, do any of you have questions?" Commence awkward pause. Awkward pause continues. "Well, since nobody has any, let's conclude for today, and I'll see you next week."

Our greatest fear with technology is that it will make us look stupid—stupid in front of a bunch of people, stupid in front of a bunch of people who are supposed to think we are smart (at least smart enough to be teaching this class). Whether it's giving a presentation at an event and our fonts get all screwed up, or like in this short story, it's in front of a small group of students, we want to share our content without hitting a snag. In this chapter, I want to "unsnag" the process of sharing content by giving you ten sharing best practices.

#1 Declutter Your Screen

When clicking on the *Share* button, Zoom is going to give us a whole bunch of choices, including every open window on our computer. While writing this chapter, I did a quick test, and the share feature gave me eight different options, plus advanced options. This array of options is necessary, but it's also overwhelming. We can rein this in by first closing all unnecessary programs and windows. In addition to simplifying things, it frees up memory and processing power on our computers. Because all video conferencing software demands a lot of resources from a computer, this decluttering is critical.

Now, it's time to tidy up the visual space on the desktop. Because it's likely you'll share your entire screen (the default option in Zoom), take some time to clean up your desktop files. Set the background to something that's not-too-busy, something that reflects who you are, and might even be a helpful conversation piece.

#2 Notifications and Messaging

Imagine teaching a class, and an email notification pops onto your screen, one that includes the name of a student facing disciplinary action. Or imagine you've left your text messaging software on, and your partner sends you a playful note—not something you want your learners reading. Before you begin using screen sharing in class, figure out how to turn off those email and text notifications and close windows that contain private information, such as student grades.

#3 Open Your Files

Before your session, open the presentations you'll be using, access the websites you'll be sharing, and any other documents or programs you'll need. Opening so many windows may sound like the opposite of my *declutter* recommendation. However, these are the essential tools you need for class, and for them to appear in your share options, Zoom needs these open *before you initiate share screen.*

Are there questions you'll send to breakout groups via Chat? Put them in a text document and have it ready so you can copy and paste the text into the chat window. Think of this as getting all your paints out on the palette before you begin painting. This little practice will impress your students, and for a few minutes in the day, someone may just believe that you've got it all together.

#4 Share for Presentation, Not Conversation

When you share the slides, a website, or a document, the screen share will monopolize the screen and reduce the number of students who are visible to you. This screen takeover is okay during lecture segments or while explaining instructions for an activity. However, the shared screen essentially hides the participants, making it difficult to have a discussion. So, if you are shifting between lecture and discussion, learn to stop the screen share when you pose a question or invite conversation.

#5 Practice, Practice, Practice

At the time of this writing, *Stop Share* is a small, red button under the floating toolbar in Zoom. This makes going in and out of screen sharing a bit difficult. Because of this, it's worth spending some time to start *Share, Stop Share, Start Share* (with the whiteboard this time), *Stop Share*...you get the point. I'd also recommend docking your Zoom toolbar to the top-right of your screen so that your controls are always in the same location as you move between the different views.

#6 Annotation

This feature allows us to markup our presentation as you talk. We can draw over top of slides or a document, spotlight portions of text, and type comments over the item we're sharing. When granted permission, students can annotate on any shared screen, document, or whiteboard. Play with annotations and consider creative ways to leverage them in your teaching. (See the companion webpage for this chapter for more on annotations.)[1]

A Brief Reflection

Let's pause here for a moment to get just a tad philosophical. Why do we share stuff in the first place? Why do we want our students to see our presentation, a short video, or to work from a shared document? Perhaps it's to visualize complex concepts and data or to illustrate a new idea. However, I believe our most deep-rooted reasons for sharing go beyond pedagogy. Our desire to share starts well before our first show-and-tell time in kindergarten. What's the first thing a child does when grandma and grandpa walk through the door for Christmas dinner? They take them right to their gifts and tell them all about them. Sharing is a human act of generosity. It's a desire for others to partake in the joy of our experience. As teachers, when we share, *we make a human connection with our students.* As you go about learning these technical ins and outs, remember that it's more than just figuring out the systems. Through sharing, I believe we are creating a more human and welcoming experience in your online classroom.

#7 Collaborative Documents.

I think this is one of the most effective ways to work with breakout groups. Fruitful breakout discussions have a clear question-set or guide for the discussion. We'll get into the nuts and bolts of this in the chapter on discussion guides, but here's the basic vision for how you can share collaborative docs. Create a Google or OneDrive doc, grab the link, and post it to your LMS or in the Chat. As the conversation progresses, students can add their insights and questions to the sheet. When you return to the plenary session, you can screen share the full document.[2] I love this as a teacher because I can *capture and see my students' learning process*. It's all right there in front of us in black and white text.

#8 Sharing Presentations

Many educators and presenters support their teaching with a slide presentation. When presenting slides through Zoom, we are simultaneously running two complex pieces of software, Zoom and our presentation program—and they don't always cooperate. This creates some limitations that we need to be aware of before presenting.

Presentation Eclipse

The main reason presentations can be problematic in Zoom is that presentation programs display in full-screen mode. In full-screen mode, your presentation fills your screen, hiding some of your Zoom controls and the gallery window of students' thumbnails. Imagine pressing a slideshow button in your brick-and-mortar classroom and all your students disappearing or shrinking into the corner of the room. That could create some serious anxiety. As I talk with educators who teach with video conferencing, **this vanishing student phenomenon is their most common frustration**. I call it *presentation eclipse*. My hope is that presentation software will eventually create add-ins and updated features to fix this, but at the time of this writing, we have to learn one key practice and employ some workarounds.

The **key practice** is to get familiar with the keyboard shortcuts that reveal all the open programs/windows on your computer. Knowing our shortcuts is essential, especially if we have a single-screen setup. In Microsoft Windows, this is the *Windows + Tab* keys, and for Mac, it's typically the *F3* key or *CMD+Tab* shortcut. These shortcuts will be how we find the Zoom window when it disappears behind a presentation.

The first **workaround is to use dual monitors**, an external monitor in addition to your primary laptop or desktop screen. In Zoom, this allows you to place your presentation on one screen and your students on the other. The dual-monitor solution will enable us to use our presentation, preserving any transitions and animations. However, it will not work with *presenter view* (more on that in a moment).

Note: Hang in here with me because these next several paragraphs get technical. I promise this is as technically complicated as the book gets. I don't like including detailed instructions like this in a book because a) they are hard to follow, b) they quickly become outdated, and c) we want to focus on the teaching more than the tech. (Feel free to scan this next segment and access the tutorials and most up-to-date information on the *Online Teaching with Zoom webpage* for this chapter).

The second **workaround is for single-screen setups**. This workaround allows you to share complete slides and view your students, but you lose slide builds, transitions, or other animations. To do this, first open any presentation created in PowerPoint, Keynote, or Google Slides. Export it as a PDF. Open the PDF, turning on the thumbnail view so that you can see a table of contents of your slides in the sidebar of your PDF viewer. Size the slides to fit within the left-half side of your screen. Now, share it using the *portion of screen* method in the *advanced* tab of *share*. Resize Zoom's green rectangle with your mouse, adjusting it to the frame the current slide.

Next, you'll want to resize the window of student's faces and place them on the right side of the screen. To do this, click on the gallery view icon at the top-right of the student thumbnails window. Now, drag the bottom corner out to expand the window and fill the right-hand side of your screen. Doing this will maximize the number of student thumbnails in the window. Your slides will now be on the left half of your screen and your students on the other half. This is my preferred way to present using a single screen because it gets the complicated presentation software out of the way and helps me to focus on teaching. I lose the fancy transitions and animations, but in most cases, those are icing on the cake, and usually of little educational value.

Presentation View/Presenter View

Many of us rely on PowerPoint or Keynote *presenter view* to view our upcoming slides and our teaching notes. If this is you, I have some bad news: *presenter view* does not cooperate well with video conferencing software like Zoom. Again, in *presentation/presenter mode*, your students will disappear. You might think that having dual monitors would fix this, but it doesn't. In *presenter mode*, the presentation overtakes *both* screens and hides your students behind the presentation. They can see you and the presentation, but you will not be able to see them. This limitation presents a significant impediment for educators who have built a high volume of material into the notes pane of their presentations.

One low-tech workaround is to print your teaching notes and work from the hardcopies, presenting using one of the workarounds mentioned above. A second workaround is more complex and requires a second computer to share content. Because this is challenging to describe in text and has multiple steps, I'll share this as a tutorial on the *Online Teaching with Zoom webpage for Chapter 4.*

A third workaround for a single screen setup will hide your students, but it allows you to see your notes while only sharing your current slide. This workaround works with PowerPoint but not with Keynote.[3] First, go into the *presenter view* of PowerPoint to initiate your slide presentation. As mentioned earlier, your Zoom window and tools will disappear behind the presentation. Use the *Windows + Tab* or Mac *F3* shortcut to find and select your Zoom Window. Next, go to *Share* on the Zoom toolbar. Next, in the Zoom sharing options, select *advanced* (at the top of the share window), then select to share *portion of screen*. You'll see a green rectangle appear over top of your PowerPoint screen. That's your active sharing window. Move it around and adjust the edges of the box to frame just the active slide area of *presenter view*. This active portion will now share only the current slide to your students.

#9 Sharing Video

With Zoom, you can share streaming video and its audio with your students. It's as simple as sharing your screen, but there is one critical item you can't forget. When you initiate *Share*, you need to select *share computer sound* at the bottom-left of the share box. If you plan to go full-screen with the video, then you'll also need to check the *optimize for a full-screen* box.

Sharing video is demanding on your computer and internet-related resources. So, make your video sharing strategic and short. I've noticed that longer videos embedded into a presentation sometimes need time to buffer. This issue may require you to play a few seconds of the video then pause it to buffer while you talk with the class for a minute or two. I recommend you provide students with links to the videos in the LMS course site, course notes, or via the chat window—that way, they have a backup to access in case sharing the video becomes problematic. I'm impressed that Zoom software can handle this kind of video sharing from both files saved to my computer or streaming from online sites. However, there are too many things that can go wrong with large video files. If you want students to view longer videos, consider requiring them to watch them before class instead of sharing them during class.

Many instructors want to use video *within a presentation*. The most straightforward approach to this is to *embed* the video within your presentation. Essentially, the embed approach allows for your video to *play inside the presentation window*. Otherwise, you must exit your presentation, go to a browser like Chrome/Firefox/Safari or a video file on your computer, locate the video, and share the video (interrupting the flow of your teaching and adding a bunch of unnecessary steps). Embedding skips this process.

Here, we need to pause for a technical sidebar: At the time of this version of *Online Teaching with Zoom*, Microsoft PowerPoint (the most popular presentation software) supports embedded online video for the PC version of their software, but not for Mac. For Mac, you have to download the video and save it into your presentation, which makes for larger files. Similarly, Apple's *Keynote* software allows you to embed downloaded videos. One helpful workaround is to use the online version of PowerPoint (Office 365), which allows users to embed a hyperlinked video.

#10 Transition with a Question or Narrate the Invisible

Even when well-prepared, we will experience dead spaces during our sharing. These are those transitional moments when we are looking for the correct file to share and trying to do it the right way. Our students can't see what we are doing, so everything goes quiet. These gaps are good occasions to ask a question and have students reflect while we transition. Another approach is to keep talking, narrating what we're doing. "Let's move on. I'm accessing a website that I want you all to see. It's a project conducted in 2008 by the National Institute of Health and..." The narration is more than filler because it provides helpful background information and the rationale for what we're preparing to share. Both practices are effective ways to maintain attention and iron out the awkward transitions.

A Final Note on Share with Mobile

The Zoom sharing process on mobile devices, like iPads, tablets, and cell phones, is still kind of clunky. This issue has more to do with the operating systems of mobile devices than the Zoom software. It's possible to share on these devices but it has real limits. If you plan to use a mobile device and have a desktop or laptop option, I'd encourage you to try it out on both and compare the experience. If you still prefer your mobile device, figure out a good workflow prior to teaching.

Sharing is one of the two features you'll use most often in Zoom. The second, and probably most important are breakout rooms, the subject of our next chapter.

5

BREAKOUT ROOM BASICS

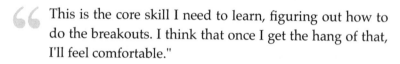 This is the core skill I need to learn, figuring out how to do the breakouts. I think that once I get the hang of that, I'll feel comfortable."

— Graduate Professor of Psychology

BREAKOUT ROOMS (what Zoom calls small-group meetings within a meeting) may be the most important technical tool in your teaching toolbox. And the larger the class, the more essential breakout rooms are for creating a conducive learner-centered teaching environment. In Part 4, we'll explore how to create and manage effective learning groups. First, we need to acquire the technical basics. In my work with instructors, I've noticed that those new to breakout rooms are hesitant to even click on that Breakout Rooms button for fear their students might disappear into the quantum realm, never to be seen again. In this short chapter, I hope that by following the steps laid out below, you'll move from hesitant to confident and ready to become a breakout room master.

How Breakout Rooms Work

I like the analogy of "rooms" because each group you create is essentially taking place in a different and separate virtual space. If Tessa, Ron, and Elodie are in Group 1, they can only hear, see, and communicate with each other. This means they will not be interrupted by other participants—unless you decide to join them. As the meeting host, you can jump in and out of different breakout rooms to listen in, coach the conversation, and answer or ask guiding questions. However, other students, from outside the group, cannot jump into other breakout rooms. In short, they are in separate spaces.

Breakout rooms first have to be enabled on your account. To do this, login to your Zoom account settings and toggle the Breakout Rooms setting to on. (See tutorial.)[1]

To practice breakouts, you'll need live participants in your Zoom session. Because of this, I recommend two things: 1) watch Zoom's tutorial video on how breakout rooms work.[2] The video gives you the student perspective so that you have a solid idea of what your learners will experience. 2) Organize a Zoom meeting with 2 to 4 colleagues or friends and work through the process of putting people in breakout rooms, moving participants, combining breakout rooms, exiting breakouts, and going back into breakout rooms.

Once in breakouts, your learners can click on the *Ask for Help* button to get your attention. I like to think of this as akin to the *Page the Flight Attendant* button on the airplane. To join one of your breakouts, click on a small *Join* button that's beside each of the Breakout Rooms (within the Breakout Room options window). If you need to send a message to all of your breakouts, such as a time-management message or follow-up question, click on the *Broadcast a message to all* button. Type and send your message.

When you end a session, the groups are alerted, and a countdown timer starts on their screens. You can make this countdown anywhere from 10 seconds to 2 minutes in the Breakout Rooms options window.

Breakout Room Best Practices

#1 Grouping Students

The last thing you want to do is waste 5 minutes of class time fumbling through the process of assigning participants to the different breakouts. The more students you have in a class, the more time it will take. There are two different approaches, and you can implement both of them quickly.

Auto-Assign

Zoom will automatically create groups for you and randomly assign participants. Just enter how many rooms you want and click on the *Create Breakout Rooms* button. A notation above the button will let you know how many participants Zoom will assign per room. Before deploying, you can adjust the group size by increasing or decreasing the number of groups. This auto-assign option is the speedy approach, best suited for: a) short, low-stakes conversations and tasks, and b) creating variety and diversity in discussions by allowing students to get to know different people.

Manual Assign

While the auto-assign feature is handy, it does not retain students in the same groups when going in and out of breakouts. To build group cohesion and sustained critical thinking, we'll need stable group membership. Thankfully, Zoom also allows hosts to manually assign groups that will maintain the same members throughout a Zoom session. Its checkbox system makes this a relatively quick task. However, there are two logistical keys to making this efficient.

- First, your students must enter their correct names into Zoom. If they enter the meeting with names like Beiber, Beyoncé, or Lebron James, you'll have a difficult time grouping your students by name. They can change their thumbnail title by clicking on their name in the participants' list or the 3-dot box in the top-right of their video thumbnail then selecting *Rename*.

- The second key practice is to create a cheat-sheet—especially if you have a large class. This cheat-sheet is simply a list of groups with the names of each participant. Don't bury this in your file system. In fact, open it before your session begins so that you can quickly bring it up and load your groups. Better yet, go old school and print off a hardcopy. Once established, Zoom will remember your groups for the remainder of the session (but it won't remember them the next time you host a meeting).

A third alternative allows you to pre-assign Breakout Rooms within the settings of a scheduled Zoom meeting through the *Breakout Room Assignment* function. You can create these manually through the interface or upload a spreadsheet (.CSV file). You can download the .CSV format and see step-by-step instructions at Zoom's online Help Center.[3] However, the pre-assign approach can be problematic because it only recognizes users who log in with the email recorded in the spreadsheet. If they enter the meeting with a different account, they will need to be assigned manually.

After employing any of these three methods, you can go in and out of Breakout Rooms without having to rebuild them.

In talking with students and reading course feedback, students prefer the stability of regular groups. They also want opportunities to get acquainted with the other classmates. So, learn to use both auto-assign and the manual methods to create the stability students need and the variety they enjoy.

#2 Reflection Time (while you build groups)

Similar to screen sharing, when you manually assign groups, you'll have a couple of minutes of dead space. We all know how this can kill the learning momentum and sometimes even derail your teaching. To remedy this, give your groups the first question prompt or initial task to reflect upon while you assign the breakouts. Have them jot down some notes to bring with them into their breakouts. Keep the question or task to a simple 1-2 minute segment and allow enough time for them to complete it before initiating the breakouts.

#3 Set a Timer

Time can speed up and evaporate during breakout sessions, especially if you're bouncing between the rooms. I use my phone's countdown timer app to notify me when it's time to end my groups. A more low-tech option is to keep a notes sheet on your desk and note the begin time of your group, and when they should conclude. I prefer the timer because I can easily get drawn into a conversation with a group and lose track of time.

#4 Combining Groups

Instead of bringing all groups back together into one large group, at times, you may want to combine two groups into a mid-sized group where they can discuss different viewpoints, share summaries, or perhaps conduct an abbreviated debate. You can do this by going to your Breakout Room assignments, hovering over each student in a particular group, then clicking on the *move to* button, and selecting the group to which you desire to move them. At the time of this writing, you still must move individuals. Finally, it's a good idea to first inform your students before moving them. Broadcast a message to let them know what you're doing and how much time they have before you move them into the combined group. That way, they don't just magically get transported into a different conversation without warning.

Those are the basics. In *Part 4: Working with Breakout Rooms,* we'll dig deep into how to teach with breakouts using active learning segments and small group learning strategies.

6

CHAT

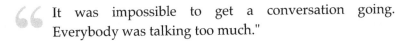 It was impossible to get a conversation going. Everybody was talking too much."

— Yogi Berra

IN ZOOM, you can hear and see each other on streaming video, so why would you need a text-based chat window? Do we really want side conversations going during class? Isn't it just a distraction from the learning process?

You can prevent students from chatting with one another, allowing them to only chat with you, the host of the meeting. However, in this short chapter, I want to consider the educational value of chat and how you can use this tool to serve your students better.

The first reason chat is valuable in a learning setting is that it allows you to communicate with students who are experiencing technical issues. Imagine you have a student enter the Zoom classroom on day one of class, and they can't get their microphone to work. A peer or support technician can communicate privately with the student in the

Chat window to help them diagnose problems and get things fixed. If it's a complex issue, the tech support person can share their phone number so that they can get connected offline to remedy the situation.

Chat also levels the internet bandwidth playing field. You may have a student who lives in a rural area or country where their bandwidth fluctuates. They may not be able to transmit video and audio but can *receive* class audio and interact by asking questions and contributing via the *Chat* window.

However, the greatest value I've found with chat is the back-channel conversation that takes place among learners. You've probably attended a webinar and seen the questions and comments pouring in while the speaker is talking. Yes, chat can be a distraction, but it can also provide you with priceless insights into your students' learning process. It can reveal their prior learning, items you may need to define, questions that could take the learning deeper, and provides opportunities for students to send resources to one another.

Here are a couple of examples.

Chat #1

Abe: You keep mentioning the importance of building mental models. What exactly is a mental model?

Charissa: I keep thinking the same thing :)

Trish: It was in our reading in Brown this week, pages 118-20

Abe: Oh…I think I skimmed that ;)

Trish: Yea, but I'm still not sure why it's so important.

Professor response after reviewing chat: "I've been assuming that the reading gave you all enough info on this concept of mental models. Review the pages Trish mentioned in the chat. But let's take a few minutes for me to explain why mental models are so important and perhaps provide you with some examples.

Chat #2

Alex: I found the HBR article on the *Bain Pyramid of Value* fascinating!

Patrick: Me, too!

Abe: I'd like to see our department at work, use it.

Trish: Same here!

Professor response after reviewing chat: Sounds like the HBR article for this week was valuable. I was planning a breakout discussion on brand partnerships, but I wonder if I'm getting a bit ahead of myself. Let's shift gears and discuss the Bain Pyramid instead.

You can see from the examples of how chat makes learning visible. It gets it out of their heads and onto the screen, helping you to uncover expert blindspots and to question your assumptions about what your learners most need. In short, back-channel chat can make your Zoom classroom more responsive and emergent.

To make this effective, you'll want to **include some basic chat protocols**. The most crucial protocol is to stay on topic. In your chat protocol, provide a couple of examples to help your students discern what passes for a legitimate chat and what's tangential.

The key teaching discipline for incorporating chat into our Zoom classroom is knowing when to check it. I like to keep the *Chat* window offscreen while I'm lecturing. After I finish teaching, I reference the chat. For instance, after 8-10 minutes of presenting new material, I say, "Okay, I'm going to take a moment to review the chat before we move on to our breakout groups. I'll be back in just a moment." This makes the minute or two it takes to scan the chat entries much less awkward for your students. It is again a good time to have your students shift into reflection mode by employing one of the shorter active learning methods described in *Part 3: Active Learning with Zoom.*

If you have a very large class or are conducting a webinar, you will likely need a teaching assistant to review, interact with, and curate the chat while you're teaching. In this case, instead of referencing the chat, you may pause after lecturing to check in with the TA or moderator, who can draw your attention to themes in the chat, or the most significant and recurring questions. Alternatively, if you don't have the resources to provide a teaching assistant for your course, you can rotate the role between your students, which can help increase their ownership and sense of responsibility for the learning community and their learning process.

Finally, it's essential to know when a tool like chat is no longer useful. You've experienced this with email. After typing several sentences into a reply, you realize that the conversation would be more efficient and effective as a phone call (or a Zoom meeting). When chat gets overcrowded, and students are typing out long responses, it's an indicator that our students are using the wrong tool. If they are that motivated to converse, then it's time to get them into breakouts for active learning segments where they can talk.

7

POLLS

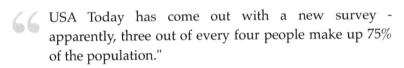 USA Today has come out with a new survey - apparently, three out of every four people make up 75% of the population."

— David Letterman

IF YOU'VE USED clickers in the classroom or a phone-based technology like *Poll Everywhere*, the Zoom polling function provides a similar feature. The Poll function in Zoom is both a useful educational tool and a great way to add variety to your class sessions and reengage the attention of your students. You can build polls to use as a quick pre-assessment at the beginning of class, a way to surface assumptions, to prime conversations, and for low-stakes quizzing. You can keep answers anonymous, allowing students to focus more on the question than on their performance or how others might perceive them, and you can share the results with the entire class (by clicking the *Share Results* button).

The most important technical thing to remember about polls is that they are attached to specific meetings. For example, if you create a poll in your Personal Meeting Room (PMI), that poll only exists in that particular meeting room. If you were to schedule a stand-alone meeting or use the Zoom LMS integration to set up unique meetings, you would need to create the poll questions within those specific meetings. I mention this because no one wants to spend time creating polls only to be in class and realize the polls were attached to the wrong meeting.

Like the other tools mentioned in this first part of the book, the best advice is to play in the sandbox. Set up a meeting or enter your personal meeting room, then go into the meeting management page for that meeting, scroll to the bottom and look for the text, *"You have not created any poll yet."* Click the *Add* button to create a poll for the meeting. This button can be a bit difficult to locate because, at the time of this writing, it's in a small font within a box and not part of a heading on the page. However, you can always press buttons *Control+F* to turn on your browser's find function and search for "poll" to locate it.

Poll questions are multiple-choice, with options that allow students to select multiple responses or a single answer. You can create polls during a meeting, but the process can be a bit clunky because it sends you out of the Zoom meeting window and into a web browser. Because of this, it's best to draft polls prior to class and strategically integrate them into your instruction.

After building poll questions, start the meeting, and click on the *Polling* button to launch your poll. If you have more than one poll, there is a drop-down arrow at the top of the polling window where you can select the different poll questions you want to use. This drop-down menu is another element that can be challenging to locate, so take a minute or two to create a few polls and practice selecting and deploying them. Click *Launch Poll* to make it go live and *End Poll* to get the results. Share the results with your students by clicking the blue *Share results* button at the bottom of the poll. Zoom saves all poll results to your specific meeting pages in your account at Zoom.us

We explore some creative ways to use polls in *Part 3: Active Learning with Zoom,* and you'll find more examples in the downloadable bonus chapters.[1]

8

SECURITY

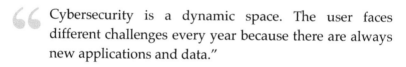

Cybersecurity is a dynamic space. The user faces different challenges every year because there are always new applications and data."

— Ken Xie, CEO of Cybersecurity firm Fortinet

WE ALL WANT A SAFE CLASSROOM. Sadly, over the last 20 years, the safe haven of our schools and classrooms has become targets and vulnerable spaces. The digital classroom is not exempt. In the Spring of 2020, when so many schools went online using Zoom and other video-conferencing platforms, we learned of "Zoombombings" where uninvited individuals accessed meetings to harass students and teachers. Other security issues surfaced, and users shifted from an attitude of implicit trust of videoconferencing technology to deep concern. Thankfully, Zoom and other providers responded and prioritized security and privacy features within their software. As stewards of our classrooms, we are responsible for keeping our virtual classroom as safe and secure as possible. This means becoming conversant with the security features and settings in Zoom.

This chapter will cover the basics. It's important to note that security features are constantly being analyzed and updated, so the best resource for learning the most current security practices within your videoconferencing platform is to visit the software's security homepage. You'll find a list of links to the security pages for Zoom and the other top videoconferencing platforms at the *Online Teaching with Zoom webpage* for this chapter.[1]

#1 Know Your Account Default Settings

If you're part of an educational institution, your Education Technology or Information Technology departments should have defined some default security settings for Zoom that align with your school's standards. A great way to get to know these is to talk with a member of your tech support team. If you're an individual user, your account will have some default settings set by Zoom. To access these settings, log in to Zoom.us, and select *My Account.* Select *Settings* from the left-hand sidebar, then select *In Meeting (Basic)* to begin working through your different meeting settings.

#2 Your In-Meeting Security Controls

To access your in-meeting security settings, first, enter a Zoom meeting, then click the security shield icon in the Zoom toolbar. These settings allow you to:

- **Lock Meeting:** When set, no other participants can join.
- **Enable Waiting Room:** This automatically puts participants in a holding area. To admit participants to the meeting, you must select their name from the participants list and admit them into the room.
- **Allow Participants to Share Screen:** If participants are allowed to share, they can interrupt your teaching with a screen share or perhaps share inappropriate images or videos. We each have to gauge the maturity level and know our participants before deciding to allow access to open sharing. If you need students

to share, then you can turn this feature on and off through the *security* or share *controls*.

- **Allow Participants to Chat:** This turns *Chat* on and off for all participants. If chat becomes problematic, this allows you to block chat use. Within your meeting controls, you can limit chat to occur only between participants and hosts. With this set, students can chat with you, but it prevents them from chatting with one another.

- **Allow Participants to Rename Themselves:** Renaming allows students to enter a name different from the name on their account. Renaming can be problematic because students can type in silly or inappropriate names.

#3 Login Using Your Institution's Account

Sometime in the past, you may have created a videoconferencing account separate from the official account established by your school or organization. Don't teach from this individual, private account. Instead, log in to Zoom, or other videoconferencing software, using your institutional account. Using your institution's account will apply your school's default security settings and place your use under the umbrella of your institution's policies. Your students should do the same, using the account provided by your organization.

#4 Removing Troublemakers

A friend was teaching a Junior High Math class when a student's behavior required her to remove the student from the meeting. A minute later, the student popped back into the meeting and began to disrupt class again. To prevent this, you'll need to turn off the *Allow removed participants to rejoin* setting. You'll find this in your account settings within the *In Meeting (Basic)* settings set.

#5 Prevent Uninvited Participants (Zoombombers)

One of the things I love about Zoom is that I can send a link to anyone and they don't have to download a bunch of software or create an account. This feature is helpful when I want to bring a guest speaker into class who may not have a Zoom account. However, this level of access creates some real vulnerabilities. It's like leaving the door open on your front porch. There are several features in Zoom that you can use to prevent uninvited guests:

- Waiting Room: This meeting control puts all participants into a waiting room when they access the meeting. The host can then admit participants individually.
- Lock Meeting: After everyone is present, then the host can lock the meeting, preventing anyone else with the meeting link from joining.
- Password Protect Meetings: In the meeting settings, you can require a password for each meeting.

In addition to these features, be discerning in how you share your meeting IDs. Sharing a Zoom meeting ID or link is like sharing your phone number. Keep this meeting information within official channels of communication, like your Learning Management System or institutional email. Avoid posting meeting links and IDs on social media or other open channels.

#6 Generate Unique Meeting IDs

Every Zoom user gets a PMI, a personal meeting ID. Think of this as your private phone number within Zoom. Because, like a phone number, this meeting identifier never changes, it's more vulnerable to access. Anyone who has used the meeting ID or link can dial into it in the future. If I were to use my PMI for all my classes, students from my 9 AM class could conceivably access my 11 AM class, and students from my Fall term courses could log into my Spring term courses. Prevent this by scheduling unique meetings and recurring meetings for different courses. The easiest way to do this is with a Learning Management System integration.

#7 Use LMS Integrations

Zoom has integrations with LMS platforms like Moodle, Blackboard, and Canvas. These enable you to schedule your Zoom meetings within your Learning Management System, and they help with security because students (depending on your LMS and Zoom settings) will log in first to your LMS before they can access the meeting links. (See Zoom's LMS integrations page for more information).[2]

#8 Disable Join Before Host

Join Before Host allows students to mill around and talk before the host arrives. This allowance may be just fine for older students, but allowing younger students to meet in an unsupervised environment can be problematic. You can switch this on or off in your meeting controls, applying the setting to all of your meetings or just to an individual meeting. When disabled, a participant will receive a pop-up box asking them to wait for the host to start the session.

#9 Decide, Don't Default, with Recording

First, familiarize yourself with your school or organization's policies for recording meetings. If you are recording, Zoom will show an alert to both you and your participants in the upper-left corner of the screen. However, it's still important to tell your students when you intend to record a session. To protect privacy, only use recording when necessary. In other words, don't make recording a default setting for your meetings. Recording also impacts what students are willing to share, so it can hinder conversation and learning.

#10 Keep your Zoom Client Up-to-Date

The *Zoom Client* is the Zoom software program downloaded onto and running on your computer. The software should push notifications to you when it needs to be updated. When you see these, update them. They will apply the latest security updates and new software features. You can also update the software by clicking on your profile in the top-right of the Zoom client, then choose *Check for Updates* from the drop-down list. I recommend using the Zoom client for all meetings because it provides users the complete set of features and functionality.

As you work through these settings, you may find some of them defaulted and locked. This is likely because your school's Zoom administrator has set them according to internal policies, preventing users from making any changes.

You have completed *Part 1: The Technical Stuff*. In *Part 2: A Recipe for Success*, we shift gears from the technical to the two main ingredients for success in the Zoom classroom. The first ingredient is understanding what learners tell us makes for good and bad videoconferencing experiences. The second ingredient is our classroom protocol document, the standards we set to help establish the culture and norms of our virtual classroom.

II A RECIPE FOR SUCCESS

- The Student Perspective
- Classroom Protocols

GOAL: to ground our teaching habits and classroom management in an understanding of the student experience of the videoconferenced classroom.

Part II

A Recipe for Success

9

THE STUDENT PERSPECTIVE

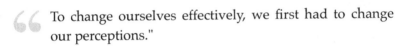 To change ourselves effectively, we first had to change
our perceptions."

— Stephen R. Covey

BEFORE WE DELVE into teaching practices, I want to ground and
frame our practices in the student experience. These pages will ask,
from the student's perspective, "What makes for a successful Zoom
session?" and "What are the common mistakes and traps we should
avoid?" I believe it's critical to start with the learner's perspective
because many of the best practices for videoconferencing assume a
meeting environment, not a *classroom* context. The student feedback that
follows will help us to reframe how we perceive and use this technology in educational settings.[1]

Recipe for a Bad Zoom Session: What Students Say Gets in the Way

#1 "Class drags when it's full of information but no conversation."

Learners log in to the videoconferenced classroom primed to talk and collaborate. And long periods of lecture feel tedious and stale in this virtual space. Students' desire for activity and discourse is not unique, but videoconferencing amplifies it because the technology was built for interaction.

#2 "Those long, awkward pauses—they are the worst."

There are some interesting technical reasons behind why videoconferenced meetings can feel so clumsy and awkward. Instead of hesitancy, students need teachers willing to practice a more assertive style of classroom leadership. They want a participative environment where their peers will "jump in and speak up." We'll address these practices in *Chapter 13: Facilitating Active Learning* and *Chapter 19: Facilitating Breakouts I - Leading*.

#3 "There's way too much content and too many activities."

This is by no means unique to the Zoom classroom. In my early years teaching, I would over-prepare, biting off more than I could chew (or my students could chew). Recently, I asked a seasoned professor, "What's different for you in this decade of teaching?" He replied, "I communicate less, probably because I think a bit less highly of my own thoughts." There is a certain pressure, especially for young teachers, to cover *all* of the content. But on the student side, this is overwhelming. Videoconferencing requires us to slow down and create spaces for interaction. If this were an equation, it would look like this: ***Slow Down + Create Interactive Spaces = Less Time for Material.*** This presents quite a challenge to those of us who are adapting our on-campus courses to the on-Zoom classroom. Similarly, well-intentioned teachers can fill the class period with disjointed learning activities that disorient and swamp students in busywork. (Download the bonus chapter on structuring your class sessions along with over twenty teaching templates at *Teaching with Zoom Bonus Materials page*.)[2]

#4 "I can tell my teacher didn't take time to figure out the tech."

There is not much to add to this one. You're reading this book, in part, because you want to become competent with the technology. Your students will notice and value the investment you're making to sharpen your technical skills.

#5 "The slide presentation boxed out our conversation."

This happens when we move our class into conversation mode but continue sharing a slide presentation. In *share* mode, student thumbnail videos remain on screen, but they shrink, and fewer students are visible. In effect, the screen share monopolizes the screen space. This limited view of students restricts their conversation. Additionally, when slides dominate the screen, we send a visual and implicit message that students should focus their attention on the presentation —not on each other. What was effective in helping students focus on our instruction becomes a hindrance to conversation.

#6 "Where are we going?"

Through years of leading groups, I've learned (mostly by making a lot of mistakes) that people are dying for someone to tell them the agenda. A good agenda consists of 1) defining the purpose of the session, and 2) providing a 2-part or 3-part structure. In other words, our students want us to answer the perennial questions, "What is our purpose?" and "Where are we going?"

#7 "There are too many (or too few) students for this to work."

A highly participative environment begins to break down when we have 12 or more learners. This threshold is important to keep in mind. However, it may be slightly higher or lower depending on the subject matter, your teaching style, and other contextual factors. Many educators attempt discussions with large groups of 12 or more without realizing they are, in fact, having a conversation with only 3-4 learners. In such cases, most students are observers. We'll look more at this in *Chapter 16: Breakout Sizes and Dynamics*.

Poorly attended sessions can also impede learning because they mitigate the diversity of voices. Small class sizes can succeed on Zoom, but they often require the appropriate teaching strategies. One way to guarantee low attendance is to make videoconferenced sessions supplemental and optional. I've only witnessed one exception to this: exam study sessions. Optional exam study sessions tend to be well attended because the class time is directly connected to a high-stakes, graded item. This has prompted me to ask, "How can I integrate major projects and other graded elements into the life of my live online classroom?"

#8 The Unmuted Noisemaker

Imagine a student eating a bag of potato chips into a live microphone. Now picture a student getting up from their chair to discipline a child —on camera. These kinds of disruptions will override any possibility of learning. However, they can be avoided by setting classroom protocols and creating a culture of self-awareness—more on this in the next chapter.

#9 Unaddressed Droners

A *droner* is a learner (or an instructor) who dominates the conversation. As a teacher, it's easy to get siphoned into attempts to manage these students. A more effective way is to establish group etiquette and a classroom culture that more naturally keeps this in check. We'll explore this in more detail in *Chapter 15: Group Etiquette* and in *Chapter 19: Facilitating Breakouts I: Leading*.

#10 Unprepared Classmates

Preparation is essential to the success of this highly participative context. When students say "unprepared," they have two different types of readiness in mind. First, they expect fellow students to test their equipment before class and learn the videoconferencing tools so that they can function unhindered in the online classroom. Second, they expect their peers to have done the advanced work necessary to have an informed and meaningful conversation in their breakout groups. **This second one is the most important factor.** In *Chapter 17:*

Zoom Preps, we'll review how to create short prep activities that set your students up well for class.

Recipe for a Great Zoom Session: What Students Say Works

The following seven student recommendations are transferrable across both on-campus and on-Zoom classrooms. However, I propose that students experience the benefits of these practices at a higher level in this virtual space.

#1 Create a Participative Environment

A fruitful academic discussion means hearing from *everyone*, or nearly everyone in the class. In large classes, giving every student an opportunity to speak can be difficult or downright impossible. But there are more ways to hear from someone than just giving them the microphone. Polls tell you what *everyone* is thinking, and breakout groups offer students to hear from *everyone* in their group.

#2 Foster Group Stability

When given a choice between group variety and consistency of group membership, students favor consistency. Maintaining group membership allows students to develop a team culture, agreed-upon expectations, and it creates that sense of trust and safety needed for more demanding academic discussions and collaborations.

#3 Practice Directive Leadership

At the beginning of a movie, film directors use an establishing shot to help the audience find their bearings. Typically, these are wide-angle shots that answer the questions, "Where am I?" and "What is going on?" Our students need the same kind of framing in the Zoom classroom. This direction and framing include several elements, all of which we'll address in Parts 3 and 4 of the book:

- Clear classroom protocols and expectations
- Assertive communication skills
- The skills set needed to facilitate groups

- Structuring sessions and creating class rhythms
- Providing preparatory exercises and discussion guides

#4 Be Curious

Students want a teacher who is both an expert and a fellow learner. They hope that we will know a lot without being a know-it-all. More than the subject matter, they want teachers who are curious *about them* and *their learning process*. This means we create space for emergent questions, and we strike a balance between pre-scripted elements and the freedom to go off-script. Students say such classes feel more "organic," and teachers report a higher sense of satisfaction when they feel grounded in a structure and remain open to serendipity. Curiosity makes this possible.

#5 Tell Me Something New

Students who come prepared to class are ready for something new. The easiest way to stifle this yearning is to rehash material they have read or viewed. While this may seem an obvious thing to avoid, the *rehash* is a persistent practice to which both novice and veteran teachers fall prey. How might we move our students beyond information and into critical thinking? And into the realm of original ideas? These are the types of questions we'll address in the upcoming chapters on teaching and designing learning sessions.

#6 Develop Quality Prompts

The quality of our learning conversations depends on the quality of the questions we ask. Students tell us they want to be challenged by questions and prompts that press to consider new perspectives and ways of thinking.

#7 Make Course Materials Accessible

Our learners need access to the materials we use in class: presentations files, articles, links, etc. We can provide these within a well-organized LMS course site or send them via email prior to class. Alternatively, we can prepare a simple text document so that we can quickly copy and paste links, questions, etc., into the chat window.

#8 Design Meaningful Learning Tasks

Busywork is death to learning. We've all been subjected to it, and we've probably all been guilty of creating it. Busywork is usually the result of a well-intentioned learning activity gone awry, one that may only need a strategic tweak and integration into the life of the course. *Chapter 12: 30 Active Learning Methods* surveys a variety of methods we can use to involve our students in the work of learning, and the downloadable bonus materials will provide you with templates to support your learning goals.

With these learner-centered and learning-centered principles in mind, we now move to the second major element in our recipe for success: our classroom protocols. These guidelines have the power to eliminate distractions, create a safe learning environment, and set a positive culture where teachers can invest more time in learning and less time in classroom management.

10

CLASSROOM PROTOCOLS

 You don't win a game by hitting the ball out of the court."

— Carlos Ruiz Zafón, *The Angel's Game*

I NEED to start this chapter by saying that I'm not a big fan of proliferating rules. At their worst, classroom policies can attempt to micromanage people and avoid the hard relational work needed to build enduring relationships. On the other hand, protocols, like those in this chapter, can help set expectations. To use a sports analogy, they draw the lines for the game we are about to play, establishing what's out-of-bounds and the agreed-upon behavior for the learning community.

Below, you'll find a set of protocols to consider for your Zoom classroom. Some of these will be more or less applicable based on your context, so I've provided a downloadable and editable document on the *Online Teaching with Zoom website* you can customize for your setting.[1] These protocols ask students to be self-aware and to take responsibility for their learning environment and technology.

#1 Make sure you have a reliable Internet connection

The keyword here is *reliable*. Shared internet at your school or work is likely robust, but a shared network at a cafe or coffee shop is not. If the person beside you starts streaming a video, and the guy across the way is uploading a huge file, then your bandwidth is going to take a nose-dive, and your video and audio quality are going to suffer. Students starting a degree program may need to get internet access installed in their home or plan other arrangements so they can secure a dependable connection. I remember teaching a course, and during our initial session, one of my students on shared apartment Wi-Fi had a technician in her kitchen installing broadband. Hopefully, your school has already communicated this requirement to distance students, but don't assume students have received the communication. Get this out to your learners early in your syllabus and pre-course messaging.

#2 Secure a quiet place where you will not be interrupted.

While speaking with teachers of an online school district, one teacher noted that her chief difficulty was *where* her students were studying. "I can see and hear the mom in the kitchen behind him and the baby brother playing on the floor. It's nice to be allowed in on the realities of home. Still, it's distracting—especially for my student and the other students." Attention and our ability to focus are at a premium—and, most of the time, within our control. Help your students think through *where* they will attend class. Though technologies like Zoom make it possible to attend from anywhere, many places are just not going to work. Ask your learners to avoid crowded coffee shops and public places. This may be necessary when a student is traveling on business, but it should be the exception, not the norm. The key feature for a good space is a door they can close. At the same time, there is a reality here that we are teaching students in *their space*, and we should expect that interruptions will happen, and we should have ways to keep our class on track when they occur. However, most of these issues can be prevented by students thinking through and applying this protocol.

#3 Test your equipment before the first class session

Provide students with the *Zoom Test Room* link and ask them to test their camera and microphone before class.[2] Ideally, students would do this before every class session and anytime they are trying to connect a new piece of hardware. They should also know how to access the Zoom link for your specific course, so they are not scrambling to find it and arriving late to class.

#4 Be on time.

Encourage students to come a few minutes early to class. If they encounter technical issues, this provides the time margin to resolve them.

#5 Turn on your camera. We want to see you.

One of the drawbacks—and benefits—to the Zoom classroom is that students can't hide in the back of the room. Because we are all on camera, we are all in the "front" of class. Some learners feel self-conscious about being on camera. That's understandable and should be noted as normal. A very few may have serious challenges with this, perhaps requiring legitimate accommodations. Overall, though, we want a level playing field, everyone showing up with their video on.

#6 No attendance while operating a motor vehicle

If your students are old enough to drive, this is going to come up. Just because it's possible to drive and attend class doesn't mean it's a good idea. I recommend that students never participate (even using audio-only mode) during a videoconferenced class.

#7 Use a device that allows you to collaborate

If your class sessions require a lot of document sharing and access to digital resources, think through whether or not smaller mobile devices will work for your students. That small screen size limits what they can do and how well they can see one another in breakout groups.

#8 Come to class prepared.

The most important factor for a successful classroom experience is that students come prepared for the session. Think seriously about building this into your course grading structure. However, the best accountability is to design interactive learning that is highly dependent upon the prep, where faking it is impossible. The positive social pressure of breakout group discussions is another great reason to leverage them in your teaching.

#9 Use good lighting, framing, and a stable surface for your camera

As we mentioned in the *Prepare Your Classroom* chapter, we should instruct students to place light sources in front and not behind them and to frame their faces at eye level. Students should place laptops on a stable surface. I've seen students in Zoom sessions lying down on couches or beds, so comfortable that they were drifting off to sleep. I believe these situations are worth addressing in your protocols because such settings both mitigate a student's ability to focus and can be distracting to others. Occasionally, students have medical reasons why they may need to lay down or recline. However, most students should expect to sit upright in a chair as they would in an on-campus classroom.

#10 You are a participant

Make this expectation explicit right from the beginning. In fact, I put this at the very top of my protocols sheet. But remember, by doing so, you are also setting the expectation that this will indeed be a highly interactive environment. I was recently at a conference where several of the speakers started by saying, "I don't like to lecture, so I expect you all to participate." Then they proceeded to speak for the entire session. We'll talk about this more in the chapters on facilitating breakout groups. Still, the teaching takeaway is that interaction won't just happen by setting this expectation. You're going to have to model this and put a lot of energy into making this a truly participative environment.

#11 To mute or not to mute?

I have felt torn on this one, but eventually, I landed on a particular point of view: I'm an **un-muter**. One of the top complaints from students in the Zoom classroom is about ambient noise from unmuted microphones. This would suggest the best protocol is for students to keep their microphones muted and to unmute them when they desire to speak. However, some helpful research from Dr. Phillip Olt, Professor at Fort Hays State University, shows that keeping microphones muted has significant, unintended impacts on students.[3] It makes them feel more distant from their peers and more likely to assume the role of observer. Muting students is like having a screen door between you and them. You can see them, but there is something in the way—and you both can feel it. At the same time, when you have twenty students in a Zoom classroom, all with unmuted microphones, the background noise can be a serious interruption.

So, what do we do? I think the best policy is a non-technical one. It's self-awareness. Establish a protocol for students to keep their microphones unmuted so that they can jump into the conversation. At the same time, ask them to be aware of any background noise or self-generated sound, and to mute their microphones when this becomes a problem. Draw their attention to the microphone symbol within their thumbnail and ask them to keep track of their status. Managing the audio of 12 or 25 people should not be your job. (Well, only in the more extreme occasions like we talked about in the chapter on *Technical Difficulties*). There are really three elements to this protocol:

1. The *self-awareness* principle. Keep your mic on and mute when background noise is unavoidable.

2. The prior mentioned *quiet place protocol*. If students secure a quiet place where they can close the door, background noise should be rare.

3. Headsets and localizing microphones. Encourage students to use a good set of earbuds, a headset, or a quality desktop microphone that has a localized pickup pattern. This means the microphone has to be close to the sound source in order to detect the sound.

A quick technical note: If a student does not use earbuds or a headset, and you play a video over *Share*, that student will probably need to mute their microphone during the video to prevent feedback. This is another great reason for students to consider using earbuds or headsets instead of computer speakers. It's not a necessity, but it helps.

#12 Be aware and attentive to how you present yourself

A teacher walked up to me and said, "Online education never ceases to surprise me!" I asked what had happened. "A guy in my class showed up without a shirt!" I shook my head. "Really?" "Yep. It really threw the other students off, making it hard to have a conversation." I've found such circumstances and individuals to be the exception. Still, it's important to include in your protocols a statement about dressing appropriately for the classroom environment. When we go to a party, a formal banquet, out to work in the garden or on the car, we match our attire for the event and tasks before us. We often do this with a mind toward others, thinking through propriety. In the Zoom classroom, I've noticed that we tend to default *to the space we are in* at home instead of the shared space of the virtual meeting. For instance, during evening courses, students in bedrooms tend to wear pajamas. PJs are appropriate for bedtime, but the "real space" in this case, is the classroom. Where we sit and what we wear all contribute to the mindset and focus we bring the learning experience.

Further, I ask students to be aware of their screens when sharing, to make sure their desktop backgrounds do not distract their peers, are appropriate for the classroom, and that they turn off notifications so that the sounds and messages do not chime in or appear on the screen. Talk with them about having *a self-aware classroom*, about the benefits of self-awareness, and how it will improve everybody's learning experience.

Bonus Protocol: Create a Silly Rule

I've been surprised by how students, both young and adult, will rally behind a silly rule. A teacher I recently learned about has outlawed the word "Bieber" from her classroom. Make a rule that "No ducks or representations of said waterfowl shall be displayed in the classroom," and your students will quickly find a class mascot. This provides an outlet for our innate desire to break the rules, and serves to build the identity of the classroom. There's a danger in giving our students a list of rules at the beginning of the term because it generates the impression that we are control freaks. A silly rule can help to override this conclusion.

Some Final Thoughts on Protocols

Keep your protocols to a one-sheet, just the front page, not front-and-back. Feel free to cheat and put it in 11pt font. You can put this in a course syllabus as an appendix. However, I recommend posting it as a stand-alone document on your LMS course site or emailing it to students before the first meeting. One way to reduce the size is to parse out the technical requirements from your protocols and put them in a separate section.

Spend a few minutes during the first class meeting to review the protocols. For any review, the key is to provide new information, especially the rationale for your rules. Emphasize the learning community and your common goals. If you are doing a single-session corporate training, a protocols sheet like this may feel excessive. In that case, abbreviate it to the 3-5 most essential items and post them as a bulleted list.

Finally, it's important to note this set of protocols are *class-level* protocols. We'll have a separate set of protocols that focus on interpersonal and group dynamics in the chapter on *Group Etiquette.*

ACTIVE LEARNING IN ZOOM

- Key Instructional Practices
- 30 Active Learning Methods
- Facilitating Active Learning

GOAL: to adapt our instruction to fit the interactive shape of the Zoom classroom by integrating and facilitating segments of active learning.

Part III

Active Learning with Zoom

11

KEY INSTRUCTIONAL PRACTICES

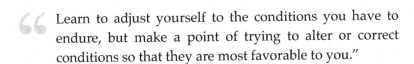 Learn to adjust yourself to the conditions you have to endure, but make a point of trying to alter or correct conditions so that they are most favorable to you."

— William Frederick

THE CORE IDEA of this book is that **Zoom was built for interaction.** Videoconferencing technologies were invented to make group *conversations* possible across great distances. Because they are interactive technologies, anytime we use videoconferencing for a sustained period, and without student interaction, we are working against the design of the tool. A second reality also impacts our teaching: In virtual spaces, we lose the familiar structures of a physical room. Because of this, the videoconferenced classroom can be disorienting and feel awkward.

In the next chapters, we'll explore practices and methods that:

1. Create opportunities for meaningful interaction (active learning)

2. Create structure in what can be a disorienting space

9 Practices to Guide Active Learning in the Zoom Classroom

#1 Agenda, Structure, and Rhythm

When a student steps into the classroom, their first question is, "What are we doing today?" As learners, we need to feel oriented. Additionally, when we are entering unfamiliar territory, our brains crave structure. Providing your students with an agenda will give them the mental shelves on which to organize the new ideas you're about to present. My personal experience is that a majority of meetings and classes lack this essential component. (You'll find more guidance for creating frameworks in the bonus material connected to this book: *Structuring Your Learning Sessions* and in the three bonus chapters of learning templates.)[1]

After we establish the structure for our session, we can begin thinking about course rhythm. **Rhythm** is applying that structure to multiple class sessions. For example, we might create a rhythm of 10-15 minutes of lecture, followed by 10-15 minutes of breakout room activities. You might be thinking, "Doesn't that get boring after a while, having the same structure?" It can. However, from reviewing thousands of course evaluations, learners say they desire predictability over variety. Our desire for stability and novelty is why musicians have established predictable formats in music, such as concertos and the chorus-refrain-bridge structure. While blues music is characterized by improvisation, most blues songs share a rather small repertoire of chord progressions. We could look to movies, novels, Broadway plays, and other art forms, and we would see the same primacy of rhythm. **Find one or two frameworks for your classroom and stick to them.** As students become familiar with these structures, they will become more comfortable to participate. When you hit this point, you'll intuitively know when to improvise and introduce variety.

#2 Active Learning Segments

Active learning is the most crucial practice in this list, and perhaps the most important practice in the entire book. Because we are conducting our class within a videoconferencing technology, students arrive primed to talk, to engage, to act. This makes extended instruction a challenge for the teacher and the learner. The next chapter provides 30 active learning methods we can employ at different points during our class sessions. Here, suffice it to say that our instruction should be punctuated by meaningful learner-centered engagement.

#3 Side-By-Side View

Your students absolutely must learn to use the *side-by-side* view. Side by side view is similar to picture-in-picture on your television. On the students' end, *side-by-side view* places your presentation (or other screen share) on the left side of the screen, and you and their fellow students on the right. A light-grey vertical line will appear in the middle of their screen. This line enables students to enlarge and reduce the size of the shared presentation. The ability to control this can be critical for those who have visual impairments and need to enlarge the text, or for those hard of hearing who need to prioritize the speaker in order to read their lips.

At the outset of your first presentation, coach your students on how to enable *side-by-side* view. It's important to know two things about this: First, because you are the presenter, *you will not see this option on your screen*. Second, your students will not be able to change their view options unless you are first sharing something. After sharing a presentation or document, direct students to their *view options* (at the top of their screen within a small green box). When they click on it, a drop-down appears. Instruct them to select the *side-by-side* view option within that drop-down. (Visit the webpage for this chapter for a demo of side-by-side view.)[2]

#4 Be Responsive

Our students learn as they, in real-time, have a chance to ask for clarifications, for further explanations, and how an idea might apply in a different situation. Good Zoom instruction is responsive. We are open to these "interruptions." Like jazz music, it's an emergent work, transformed by our students' questions. If you have taught asynchronous online courses, you probably miss this sense of serendipity. It's possible again in the Zoom classroom, but **there is one technical**

reality that will make or break responsiveness: those mute settings we touched on in the *Classroom Protocols* chapter.

Most sources encourage us to mute our attendees. I'm going to recommend the opposite. If you want responsive, back-and-forth conversation during your class session, then instruct your students to stay **unmuted** and encourage them to jump in as ideas rise to the surface of their minds. At first, they will hesitate. The hesitancy eventually shifts as you encourage students to participate and permit them to interject their questions and musings. A fellow teacher puts it this way, "I have **had** to shift to having my students keep their mics unmuted. I know some profs want quiet, but there is *so* much more direct back-and-forth between students when they are all unmuted and open to each other."[3]

#5 Higher Level of Energy (and Breaks) are Required

Teaching in this format is more demanding. When I talk with my colleagues about what it's like to teach with Zoom, they say, "Compared to my on-campus classes, this requires me to bring a lot more energy to the classroom." Psychologist Curt Thompson reflects on this in his article, "A Body of Work" Thompson notes that in-person communication requires less conscious cognitive work to interpret and understand the non-verbals of tone and body language.[4] Thompson reflects that in videoconferences, "the conscious, cognitive domain of my mind is having to do much, much more work than it is used to doing." This cognitive demand has several implications for our teaching. First, we need breaks and movement.

Second, our students need breaks and opportunities to get up and move around. Active learning segments not only support student learning, but they also offer you short windows to rest and collect your thoughts. They give students a chance to take a more active and participative role in their learning. Moreover, the active learning segments provide educators with real-time evidence that our students are learning, which in turn fuels our energy and motivation.

Because the Zoom classroom requires more energy, it stands to reason it requires strategic breaks. Thompson explains that our bodies are

made for movement. Not only do we need a rhythm of breaks, but we also need to use those breaks to move around. Encourage your students to take a short walk around the block during breaks. As you think about your own teaching space, you'll find it helpful to shift between standing, sitting, and freeing yourself to move around within the frame of your camera and the reach of your audio.

#6 Edit Your Instruction

Perhaps the most frustrating aspect of transitioning to the Zoom classroom is that it requires a slower pace. Consequently, we must adjust our expectations for how much material we can work through during a given class session. We don't have to throw out our material wholesale, but *we must edit*. We've all been in classes where our teacher was racing through information and right past our cognitive capacity to keep up. Albert Einstein once said, "Everything should be made as simple as possible, but not simpler." Einstein's words are a reliable maxim as we review and edit our material before teaching.

 Learning is deeper and more durable when it's effortful. Learning that's easy is like writing in sand, here today and gone tomorrow."

— Peter C. Brown, *Make It Stick: The Science of Successful Learning*

#7 Normalize Effortful Learning

Active learning is effortful. That's a good thing because effort is correlated with increased learning.[5] Effortful learning tends to be more durable learning. Students often resist active learning because it feels more demanding. Some students will complain, assuming that the teacher is shirking their job by making the students do the work. A study published by the National Academy of the Sciences explains, "Instructors report that students dislike being forced to interact with one another, they resent the increase in responsibility for their own learning, and they complain that "the blind can't lead the blind."[6] The authors of the study go on to say, "More recent literature shows that if instructors explain and facilitate active learning, student attitudes toward it can improve over the course of a semester."[7]

First, we should expect this response from our students. Second, we can normalize the effortful nature of real learning by appealing to other areas in life where this is true: physical exercise, building relationships, or learning to play an instrument. All of these, at times, require effort. It's in those moments that we grow, and because of that effort, we experience the most long-term benefit.

#8 Make Shared Documents Available on your Course Site via your LMS

Students regularly tell us they want to print off presentations and class notes so that they can take their notes on the hardcopies. Others may download the file and add notes as digital annotations. **They want to work with the material.** Though it's a low-tech interaction, it's an important one for retrieval of learning and aids students in their ability to stay attentive in class. I've encountered many educators who believe providing their presentation files before class short-circuits discovery in the learning process. There is some truth to this. However, I've concluded that learners' desire to take notes on these materials during class outweighs the benefits of withholding them until the end of class.

Perhaps you are in a training environment and don't have an LMS (Learning Management System, such as Canvas, Moodle, or Blackboard). In this situation, you can send the documents to your learners via email before your training session. You can also share documents through Zoom's *Chat* feature, by clicking on more (in Chat) and use the share file option.[8] (This has to first be enabled in your meeting settings).

Students usually need a more permanent way to access digital files, so I'd recommend first using your LMS for document sharing, especially with course-critical docs like study guides and rubrics. However, the Zoom document sharing function allows us to send students just-in-time resources during class. Chat is also a great way to send links to the books and websites you reference. I find it helpful to delegate link sharing to a student who can look these up and send them via chat to everyone during class. Delegating this to students helps teachers keep focused on the work of teaching. Moreover, the fact is, I usually forget to send them after class.

#9 Optimize your Audio

Mediocre audio is okay in a short presentation, but after about an hour, it becomes irritating and an impediment. For the more technical information on optimizing your audio, see *Chapter 1: The Equipment*. On the non-technical side of things, keep a glass of water on your desk and have cough drops nearby if your throat becomes irritated. Just be sure to avoid the smacks and teeth clacks that can come with cough drops. Vocal quality is one of the most natural things for a teacher to overlook simply because we don't hear our own voices as they are processed through our equipment. Because of this, **ask your students to rate the audio quality** on a 1-10 scale and find ways to get it to an 8.

In the next chapter, we shift from practices to methods. It contains 30 active learning methods organized by when they might best fit into your instructional flow.

12

30 ACTIVE LEARNING METHODS

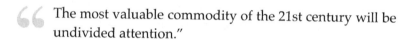 The most valuable commodity of the 21st century will be undivided attention."

—Producer Phil Cooke, author of *One Big Thing*

ATTENTION DETERMINES OUR STUDENTS' capacity to learn. We can grab their attention with a hook, but it's easy to lose their attention over the course of an hour, and even more difficult to maintain during longer class sessions. To make this even more challenging, in the Zoom classroom, we compete with stimuli in our students' homes and offices, the preoccupations of their day, distracting email notifications, and the open browser tabs on their computers. Without methods to recover and reset attention, their minds wander and become disengaged. The most effective solution is to **punctuate our instruction with segments of active learning.**

While active learning helps solve this attention problem, there is a better reason to augment our teaching with these short activities: students comprehend and retain more of what they learn when they are active participants.[1] What follows are 30 active learning methods you can employ throughout your instruction. I've arranged these to fit with the pivotal points of instructional flow: starting class, middle of class, and concluding the class session.

Active Learning Strategies for Starting Class

A learning activity can jump-start class by immediately putting students into the driver's seat of their learning. It's also a powerful way to get a sense of their prior learning so that you can calibrate your instruction to the specific needs of the class. Additionally, active learning, using specific methods, such as *In the News* or the *Sticky Scenario*, can be effective ways to establish the relevance of the subject matter.

#1 Polls

Because the polling tool is built into Zoom, it is relatively easy to set up and employ. Use polls to test comprehension by opening class with a quick, 3 to 5-question, ungraded quiz. Design these quizzes to assess whether or not students grasp the main concepts in the required reading or other preassigned material. Another approach is to create a short scenario and require students to choose from a multiple-choice list of possible solutions.

#2 Bring Questions

Ask your students to prepare for class by bringing a question that emerged from their reading or perhaps from work on a major paper or project. Invite your students to interject questions when they are most pertinent to the current material. This method is best used throughout the class period but can be a great way to start class. It gets the session underway with an inquiry mindset instead of an information mindset.

Quick Tip: You'll notice Zoom has a *raise-hand* feature in the *participants* panel. While a great idea, I find this impossible to monitor. *Reactions*, like the thumbs up and applause emojis, overlay the video and are more noticeable. However, you have to first define how to use them as there is not yet a *raised hand* emoji. In the previous chapter, I advocated for an interruptible classroom culture where students are free to interject. However, depending on the age and maturity of your students, that may not be possible. In that case, substituting the *applause* reaction emoji to symbolize a raised hand is probably the most effective option.

#3 In the News

Prior to class, your students search the news using keywords related to the class topic. Begin the class by asking a few students to screen share an article, provide a summary, and explain its connection to the material. Alternatively, place students in small groups and have them share their findings. Visit some of the groups so that you are aware of the articles and make reference to them during your instruction.

#4 Define Success

Provide your students with an outline for the class session, put them in breakout groups, and ask them to discuss, "What would make today's class a success for you?" Or make this an individual reflection with the following instructions, "Take 2-3 minutes to review the outline and get a sense of what we'll address today. Then write out a personal learning goal." Defining the goal helps students to personalize and take ownership of their role in the learning process.

#5 Comprehension Test

Comprehension tests are similar to polling but graded. One of my graduate school professors used this method for every class. He began class with a 12-15 question quiz on the core concepts of our assigned reading. When complete, we would review the questions and correct answers. During the review, he opened the floor for clarifying questions, and he would lecture only on the material that needed further explanation, ideas we wanted to explore, or theories we didn't yet understand. While Zoom polls can record individual answers, it's a lot of work to get poll results out of Zoom and into your LMS for grading.

Instead, I recommend you use the quiz module built into your LMS. These quiz modules have more robust question features, review options, and the grades will go directly into your online gradebook.

#6 Prior Knowledge Survey

Prior knowledge surveys differ from polls because they require students to write or type short essay-type responses. The most straight-forward method is to give students 2-3 minutes to write out everything they already know about a topic. You can stop there, or ask them to elaborate, going beyond the reading to make connections with their life experience, other classes, documentaries they have watched—anything is fair game. A third phase is to underline or circle what they believe is most relevant, thematic, or important. After writing, either put students in breakout groups to share what they've circled and under-lined or ask a few individuals to share with the entire class.

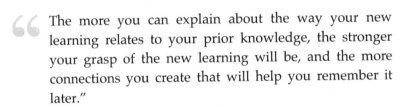

The more you can explain about the way your new learning relates to your prior knowledge, the stronger your grasp of the new learning will be, and the more connections you create that will help you remember it later."

— Peter C. Brown, *Make It Stick: The Science of Successful Learning*

#7 What's on Your Mind?

The *What's on Your Mind?* exercise is helpful when the entire class is experiencing something of cultural, personal, or institutional impor-tance that would otherwise distract them. This activity integrates the elephant in the room into the substance of the class session. Start with triad breakout groups and ask students to share what's top-of-mind for them as they begin class. The question is simple but powerful: "What's on your mind?" Sometimes this is better done in a large-group setting, but the drawback is that you only have time for a handful of students to share.

At the time of this writing, we are experiencing the COVID-19 pandemic. An instructor I work with noted that his students were experiencing a high level of anxiety. In response, he started class with a similar exercise and discovered that many of them were worried about completing their internships—a requirement for graduation. While this may have taken away valuable instructional time, it helped to reframe his instruction and to support students in ways that extended beyond the classroom and further their professional development.

#8 Learning Journals and Journal Reviews

Journals provide students an active outlet while listening to their teacher's instruction and a place to record their thoughts. One of the other benefits of journal-during-lecture is that it gives more restless students something to do. One of my friends is a brilliant high school English teacher. He can't sit still in a teacher meeting to save his life, so he doodles. It helps him to listen and pay attention.

The key to making journals like this work is to provide a set of sample prompts.

- Note things that most interest you
- Jot down questions—even if they feel unrelated
- Doodle concept maps, create lists or illustrate ideas
- Just take notes

If you make this a regular practice in your classroom, you can use journals as a reference point for most other learning activities. An especially effective way to use journals is to begin class by asking students to review their journal entries from the previous class session. Then place students in breakouts to make this a short social learning time. If you want to spend a bit more time here, ask students to make connections between their journal entries and the specific material to be addressed in the current class session. This task will help them connect prior knowledge with the new content.

#9 Sticky Scenario

The *Sticky Scenario* is my favorite activity on this list. The only drawback is that it takes more time and effort to develop. Begin class with a scenario. Embed in the scenario two to three core concepts you plan to address in your instruction. A scenario differs from a case study in that scenarios are usually imagined and contain less detail. Cases typically draw from real-life circumstances. Like a case, the scenario has to be *sticky*, complicated enough that students cannot default to easy answers. These are often ethical questions and complex problems that require students to stretch into higher-order thinking skills.

In breakout groups, give students several minutes to discuss the scenario, to surface questions, and talk about how they might approach a solution. *The goal here is not to solve the problem as much as it is to understand what's going on.* After small group breakouts, return to the large-group setting. Begin your large-group time by allowing students to ask clarifying questions about the scenario. During the teaching segments, use the scenario as an anchor point, referring to it often, allowing it to unfold, and making connections between the scenario and your content.

Quick Tip: You can employ a majority of these methods as either individual or group activities. Group activities take more time. So, if you feel pressed for time, consider retaining a learning activity, but recasting it as an individual exercise.

Active Learning Strategies for the Middle of Class

Some of the following methods can be used as informal checks to get a quick appraisal of whether or not your learners are comprehending the core concepts of your instruction. Others offer your students opportunities to reinforce their learning through such actions as summarizing, illustrating, elaborating, or sharing. Additionally, many of these activities encourage students to enter short periods of inquiry and to ask clarifying questions.

#10 Backchannel Chat

During a lesson, direct students to use Zoom's chat panel to ask questions and communicate their ponderings. You'll need to first establish protocols for this form of communication; the most important is to keep contributions on-topic. The key to making backchannel chat successful is to review it at regular intervals and to use it as a jumping-off point for short stints of large-group discussion. Reviewing the chat takes time, so while you look over it, give your students a 2-3-minute journal prompt. If you have longer class times, review the questions during breaks, and address the questions when the class resumes.

#11 Peer Instruction (an abbreviated version)

Harvard physicist and professor Eric Mazur and his colleagues developed this active learning strategy. Mazur discovered his students were leaving semester-long physics classes with the same misconceptions they had before taking the course. He found that student-to-student discussion had the power to shift this. Why? Because students could discuss and convey complex ideas in language their peers could understand. Essentially, peer instruction helps eliminate our expert blind spots. In an article in *Harvard Magazine*, Mazur explains that "Peer-instructed students who've actively argued for and explained their understanding of scientific concepts hold onto their knowledge longer."[2]

What follows is an abridged approach to this method. (Download the *Online Teaching with Zoom bonus material* to review a full Peer Instruction teaching template.)[3]

Start with a brief teaching segment. Then launch a one-question poll that tests a key concept from your teaching. Next, put students into breakout groups of two to three to discuss their answers for 3-5 minutes, where they explain to one another the thinking that led to their choice. Poll the students again to see how their responses may have changed. Reveal the polls and discuss the results, then move on to the next brief lecture.

Tips for abridged Peer Instruction:

- Integrate versions of the peer instruction questions into your exams or other assessments. This will create accountability for learning and boost student motivation to study.

- Peer Instruction is most effective when students come to class after completing the assigned reading or other required course materials.

#12 Muddiest Point

Activities #12 through #15 are informal checks. You can use these as springboards for brief large-group or small group breakout discussions. We start with the *Muddiest Point* activity because it's a classic, go-to method. The idea is simple: after an instructional segment, ask students to share what is unclear or confusing. But a critical point is often missed: *reflection*. Provide your students 1-2 minutes to consider the question. You can leverage journals by asking students to record these in their notes or to devote a section in their journal as an ongoing list of muddiest points. Muddiest points are valuable because they expose student learning gaps, providing you insights into what ideas you may need to revisit before moving on to more complicated or new content.

#13 Red Light, Green Light, Yellow Light

One of my colleagues uses an informal checks system that goes beyond the muddiest point. His system uses *red light* for ideas or perspectives students disagree with or dislike, *green light* for things they agree with or like, and *yellow light* for muddiest points. These can be journaled or shared in large-group discussions and smaller breakouts.

#14 Thumbs Up, Thumbs Down, Thumbs Sideways

I think of this as the speed method of informal checks. The *thumbs* method gives you an instant visual response from your students (if they all fit on the screen). The key is to define what the thumb positions mean: are they an agree/disagree continuum? Or are they a clarity/muddy continuum? The strength of this visual method is that you can ask a specific student about their response. For example, "Claire, you had a thumb-sideways. Would you be willing to explain why?" Because this activity is so visual, screen size will limit your ability to see the student responses. If you have more students than can fit on one screen, you may want to employ the next method.

#15 Polls for Informal Checks

You can use polls to gather and visualize informal checks. This can be as simple as a poll question with *agree/disagree/neutral* options or *red/green/yellow light* options. The benefit is that you can share the poll with your students and move the conversation according to their responses. For example, "Wow, 74% of you disagreed with the author's assertion that...Let's take a few minutes to explore why." This method is especially helpful in large settings like webinars or classes with over 50 students.

#16 Think-Pair-Share

Like *Muddiest Point*, *Think-Pair-Share* is a quintessential active learning method. I think of it as a meta-method because we can adapt its overall structure to a thousand different purposes. The key practice (too often skipped) is to *allow your students a minute to reflect* on a question or their notes. After the think time, pair students into breakouts to share their thoughts. Keep these brief, to about 2-3 minutes. If you want to maintain the same groups throughout the class meeting, you'll need to manually assign students to breakout groups.

#17 Journals

We've already explained journals in #8. In the middle of your instruction, you can pause students to reflect and write, ask what has come up in their entries, *Think-Pair-Share* their entries, or post something to the chat from their journals that they find relevant or important.

#18 Short Writes

The short write is sometimes called the *One-Minute Paper*. Students write a speed-essay, summary, or elaboration on the lesson they have just heard. Short writes can focus on such things as:

- Applications
- Explanations
- Reasons: 2-3 reasons why...
- Implications: If this is true, then...
- Elaborations
- Connections: "How does____relate to____?"

#19 Illustrate

Sometimes it helps to break free from the analytical tendencies of note-taking and journaling to draw out and illustrate ideas. Instead of a *One-Minute Paper*, have students sketch out their thoughts. Students can sketch these out on a piece of paper or use the Zoom whiteboard in breakout groups. Share the drawings in large or small groups and discuss the different ways students visualize and portray their thinking.

#20 Short Team Tasks

Send students into breakouts to complete a short task. The key is to keep the task achievable within the set timeframe. Keep it short, 3-5 minutes. Here are a few task ideas:

- Create an outline based on their notes
- Create a summary slide
- Draft a speed concept map
- Make a meme with a meme generator
- Assess a scenario and come to a decision.

Back in the large-group setting, have a representative share the product with the entire class.

#21 Phase Solutions

Phase solutions take longer because they involve 1) a small amount of deliberation, followed by 2) analysis. In breakout groups of 3-5 learners, students work through a brief case study, problem, or scenario. After coming to their decision, they outline their *decision-making process*. It's important to emphasize they are not outlining the reasons why they made their decision, but the phases of their process toward the solution. Phase solutions are helpful exercises for STEM courses, advanced math story problems, and business case studies.

#22 Abridged Jigsaw

The Jigsaw Method is more than a teaching tactic. Educators developed the model in the 1970s as a way to integrate racially diverse and previously segregated classrooms.[4] The complete Jigsaw method is explained in more detail in the teaching templates segment of this book's free bonus material. Here we'll use an abridged form because it's better suited for shorter segments of active learning.

Before or after an instructional unit (more than 15 minutes), create *expert groups* of 3-5 students, assigning each group a different aspect or perspective of the overall topic you've addressed or will address in your lesson. For example, let's say we are teaching on *Maslow's Hierarchy of Needs* in an Organizational Psychology course. Give each *expert group* a different segment of the hierarchy: physiological, safety, belonging and love, esteem, and self-actualization.

Next, give each group a question prompt they can discuss within a 10-minute timeframe. The final phase is to bring the large-group back together and have a representative from each group present a synopsis of their discussion. These succeed when the question prompts challenge students to work through implications, applications, or a short case. The unique feature of this method is that it provides each group an opportunity to do a brief but deep dive on one topic or perspective. The large-groups provide time to synthesize those diverse and sometimes differing points of view.

#23 Large-Group Discussion

In this book, I'm defining *large-groups* as groups that include the entire class or any group containing more than 12 learners. Large-group discussions have built-in limitations of time and communication dynamics. They gravitate toward a hub-and-spoke model of interaction. The dialogue is predominantly between the teachers and a handful of individuals, with limited student-to-student interaction. In large-group discussions, the teacher is the hub of the conversation, so we experience more dynamism than our students. The hub-and-spoke dynamic can create an illusion of engagement. Because a majority of students may experience large-group discussions as observers, it may not be active learning. The next chapter, *Facilitating Active Learning*, includes some guidance for facilitating this type of large-group conversation.

Active Learning Strategies for Concluding Class

The concluding minutes of class may be the most important in our instruction because of our brain's need to consolidate what we have learned. These last seven methods can help students integrate prior learning with new learning, create connections to future learning, and move students toward high-order thinking.

#24 Summaries and Takeaways

Writing summaries may appear a rudimentary task, but this very basic strategy helps students synthesize and comprehend new material. Takeaways differ from summaries because they are less about the information and more about the *impact* of the subject matter on the learner. Takeaways are explanations of those *ah-ha* or *lightbulb* moments.

#25 Concept Mapping

At the end of class, have students work alone with a piece of paper, or in groups with the Zoom whiteboard, to create a concept map of the lesson material. The second phase of this activity involves drawing lines between elements on the map to indicate connections. In a third phase, students define those connections by writing or typing along their connecting lines. During the fourth phase, students reflect on themes or new understandings that became apparent during the activity. We can abridge the *Concept Mapping* activity by using just the initial stage or stages of the process.

#26 Post Test

Whether graded or ungraded, post-tests add a sense of accountability for learning. Because such a high number of students experience test anxiety, I prefer to make these ungraded or very low-stakes assessments—especially if used often. Anonymous polls are a great way to implement post-tests.

#27 Create Test Questions

Test Questions is a more collaborative form of the *Post Test*. Similar to the *Abridged Jigsaw,* assign a sub-topic to each group and require them to create a slide with one or two post-test questions. Groups should create these slides in a program outside of Zoom, such as PowerPoint or Google slides. When they return to the large-group, each breakout group shares their slides and questions via the *Share* function.

#28 Forecasting

Forecasting is the inverse of prior learning and is particularly helpful in classes where students have significant amounts of reading that might take them beyond the topic of the current class meeting. In a short write or short breakout discussion, students work through prompts, similar to the following examples:

- How does _____ relate to next week's or tomorrow's material?
- Next week we move into _____. How is what you've learned today foundational for that next topic?
- This week we've been talking about _____. Next week we'll examine a couple of case studies about _____. What from today will help you work through those case studies?

#29 Error Identification

Think of this as a sophisticated *Where's Waldo?* activity. Provide your students with brief examples or scenarios where something doesn't fit, doesn't work, or went wrong. Then ask them to identify the mistake or error. *Error Identification* tests comprehension and can require students to use higher-order thinking skills to complete. This method is especially helpful for students in professional programs learning processes, such as nurses practicing patient surveillance or counselors practicing a referral process.

#30 Application or Analysis Scenario

As you conclude class, assemble students into breakouts to work through scenarios where they must apply their new learning to a scenario or analyze a short case. These move students into higher-order thinking and can serve as informal assessments.

The key to making an *Application Scenario* successful is to use *how questions*.

- How would you fix this?
- How would you set up the experiment?
- How could we use Maslow's Hierarchy of Needs to inform how we implement this policy?

An *Analysis Scenario* requires students to identify parts of the scenario and differentiate root causes from consequences. Here are a few ideas for setting up a successful *Analysis Scenario*.

- Provide students an outline of an argument.
- Give students a link to a short reading, video, or other examples to analyze.
- Use two contrasting examples or scenarios and ask students to identify the differences.
- Provide two solutions to the same problem, then have students identify the differences in both the approach and possible consequences.
- Provide a problem. Ask students to identify the root causes and the resulting consequences.

With these 30 tools in your active learning toolbox, it's time to shift again from method to practice. In Chapter 13, we'll focus on how to facilitate these types of active learning sessions in the Zoom classroom.

13

FACILITATING ACTIVE LEARNING

 All genuine learning is active, not passive."

— Mortimer Adler, Founder of the Great Books Program

IT'S CHALLENGING to facilitate active learning. Time is of the essence, and we feel a great deal of pressure to make progress through our material. So, we want these alternating segments of student interaction to be **concise and effective**. The ten practices in this chapter will help us make the most of our limited time so that we can create a more vibrant and engaging classroom experience.

10 Practices for Facilitating Active Learning in Zoom

#1 Be Strategic with Activity Types

Because short learning activities are so adaptable and easy to employ, it's natural to use them in an ad hoc fashion, without thinking through their educational purposes. In this approach, we typically have four modes of instruction, each with their own set of strengths and limitations.

- Lecture
- Individual activity
- Small-group activity
- Large-group activity

The key practice is to align activities with our goals and time limits. It's easier to manage the clock with direct instruction and individual activities. Because of this, when speed is more critical than processing, these will be our go-to methods. Large-group and small-group activities require more time and facility to guide conversation, but they provide students with opportunities to metabolize complex ideas. Moreover, small-group breakouts create spaces for more students to talk. By contrast, while large-group discussions limit the conversation to a few individuals, they also encourage students to synthesize the work of small-groups. Large-groups are useful for conducting informal checks and making clarifications before proceeding to new material. While small-group activities require more planning, large-group activities probably require more in-the-moment leadership from the teacher to direct the flow of conversation.

#2 Leverage Breakout Groups

As we've seen, active learning can be done by individuals in short writes, journals, informal checks, polls, etc. However, active learning in a small group allows students to hear from peers of different ages, gender, and cultures. The variety of backgrounds and life experiences enrich the discourse. Perhaps most important, our quiet students, who tend to feel more nervous about speaking up in large-groups, find smaller breakouts a safe place to share and converse.

Give breakouts a time limit, clear instructions, and a *single question or short task*. Even with short scenarios or cases, the instructions should be concise, asking only one question or requiring a single decision. However, there are occasions where you may want your learners to work through a series of short questions. For this, I recommend the following process: 1) ask a single question, 2) return to the large-group to debrief, 3) send students back into breakout groups with a second question, 4) repeat.

> ...brevity is the byproduct of vigor."
>
> - William Strunk and E.B. White

#3 The Succinct Expectation

Both large-group discussions and small-group activities require teachers and students to be **concise** with their speech. This requirement can create anxiety for some students, especially those who are verbal processors. It helps to emphasize that we are all figuring this out together. (Most teachers are not exactly succinct people; we like talking—and writing long parentheticals in our books.) For adult learners, it helps to explain how speaking is a vital professional skill. Those who learn to speak with clarity grow their influence within organizations and teams. It also helps to demonstrate just how much can be said in a few seconds. Read aloud to your class the first half of the Gettysburg Address, and note that it takes only 30 seconds. The entire thing takes just over one minute. We can say a lot in a short period. The harder part is forming our thoughts before we speak them. That brings us to our next practice, *Pause to reflect*.

#4 Pause to Reflect

Unless we need immediate, visceral responses, we can create space for our students to reflect before speaking. Most of the time, this only requires a 30 to 60-second pause, but almost every active learning segment needs this supporting work of pondering. Ask students to reflect for a while before responding to a poll. Pause small-groups to stew on a question for a minute before talking. Initially, silence can be uncomfortable, but that quickly changes when we make these quiet spaces a regular practice in our classroom.

> From the quiet reflection will come even more effective action." —Peter Drucker

#5 Model Thinking and Discourse

Like pausing to reflect, we support student learning by **slowing down to make our thinking explicit**. When a teacher says, "John, what you just said connects in an important way to what Amber was explaining," the teacher is verbally connecting ideas. Think of this as narrating the conversation and bringing meaning to the discourse. In large-group debriefs, we have the opportunity to integrate the potpourri of thoughts coming into the discussion from individuals and small groups. Whiteboarding takes this narration a step further by creating a visual account of our thoughts. *How* we respond and talk, *how* we take the time to summarize what a student struggled to explain, models kindness and respect, and goes a long way in building the classroom culture we desire.

#6 Be Assertive

The videoconference classroom can feel like a busy intersection where the stoplights have gone out. Our students need us to step out into the busy street to direct the traffic. Because most of us want to be accommodating and considerate, a more directive leadership style can feel overbearing and autocratic. However, we can be assertive and polite at the same time.

A colleague of mine explains this well: "I encourage my students to speak up, interrupt me at times, and I want to make sure *everyone* is willing and motivated to have their voice heard. If this doesn't occur, then the class becomes a jumble of students unmuting, saying something, me replying, student muting again, and everyone staring at each other, waiting for someone to unmute and say something."

If you read into the next segment on discussion-based and collaborative learning, we'll explore the reasons for why the stoplights feel broken and the specific skills of pacing and interrupting that help direct the conversational traffic.

#7 Use Student Names

The most valued word to any human being is their name. During my first year of teaching, a master teacher advised me to learn the names of all 83 of my sophomore students. I grabbed a yearbook, copied the pages, and made flashcards. I'll never forget the looks on their faces when students walked through the door, and I greeted them by name. Not only did it make a powerful first impression, but it also communicated that I valued them and had a desire to know them. Zoom puts student names right on the screen below their video. It's a cheat sheet in every session, making it easy to call on students by name. This practice may be the best way to employ the *be assertive* principle. Instead of saying, "Does anyone want to share?" and wait through the awkward pause and fears of talking over one another, say, "Diane, would you be willing to share your thoughts on this?" When you see a student drifting or disengaged, use their name in an example. "So, if Lindsey were seeing a client like this, what might she do to help in this situation?" It prevents calling them out directly but immediately reengages them when they hear their name.

#8 Communication Expectations

Let's go back to the broken stoplight metaphor. At an intersection, even when the stoplight malfunctions, there are expectations for who goes next. We save energy directing traffic by setting some expectations around how to communicate. These will be different depending on your context, and some will change depending on the type of discussion. However, here are a few examples:

- If you were the first to speak in the previous discussion, allow someone else to speak first in the next discussion.
- For those of you who are more reserved, I want you to speak up, but I know you prefer to have some time to think about the question. I will call on you, but I will also try to do so *after* giving you some time to think over the question.
- You are always free to pass when I call on you.

#9 Commit to Sharpening Your Large-group Skills

The most demanding context for active learning is the large-group setting. In large-groups, we experience rapid-fire interactions. We endeavor to encourage freedom in the conversation while guiding talk in a meaningful direction. Facilitating large-group discussion is a demanding task and requires a skill set that includes: rephrasing, summarizing, gently interrupting, connecting ideas, thanking and appreciating, using names, giving space to think, pacing the conversation, concluding, and transitioning. These are all skills we can sharpen.

Two approaches can aid us in this effort. The first is to pick a single skill that we desire to improve in each Zoom session and to be attentive to it. Simply noticing is usually enough to catch our attention and make focused improvements. In short, this need not be a significant undertaking. But there are some habits we cannot improve because they are in our teaching blindspot. We all can recall the annoying habits of our high school teachers, the quirks no one told them about, but everyone would imitate. Coffee breath is, thankfully, not an issue on Zoom, but we have less-glaring mannerisms and habits that will not change without feedback. Be brave and ask students to give you feedback on how you can improve. We'll look more into how to do this in *Chapter 20: Improving Our Game.*

#10 Acknowledge the Limits of Conversation

Let your students know that most large-group will be teacher-to-individual student, a hub-and-spokes format of communication. Breakout groups will be the exception, but the time in small-groups goes by quickly. Often, the conversation will feel like it's just getting started, then is cut short by the need to move on to the next topic. This limitation is important to forecast because some students can become frustrated by these brief opportunities to talk. However, if we first communicate our expectations and the limits of our teaching methods, our students will adjust and learn to function within the time frames and purpose of these groups.

However, there are times when our students stretch the limits of our teaching methods to the point where our go-to methods no longer fit. The next chapter will help us diagnose when it's time to consider new methods and perhaps different paradigms for teaching and learning.

INTERLUDE: ADAPTING

Because Zoom requires us to adjust our teaching habits and adapt our material, we can feel stretched and begin to encounter the limits of our go-to pedagogies. Sometimes other factors outside our control force us to reconsider our methods. This happened to me when an online course I taught doubled in enrollment. I had built my teaching around teaching a class of 20 students. Now, I had 40 students in one online course.

First, I did what every responsible and caring teacher would do: I freaked out. After regaining composure, I realized I needed to reconsider what had become my normal mode of teaching. Reading up on group-based collaborative learning methods, I employed a project-based learning model (PBL) and divided my students into ten working groups. This required shifts in how I thought about learning and my role as the teacher. It also required changes in how I structured and prepared for class, a shift from supporting individuals to supporting *teams*. And it changed how I would assess student work. Though it was demanding and stretching, it was probably the most significant moment in my teaching career. In this new format, my students surpassed my expectations. This was not an AP course, but in several cases, these high school seniors were doing college-level work. This paradigm shift didn't mean I had to throw out my former practices. Instead, it added new tools to my teaching toolbox.

I believe that **videoconferenced learning is impacting many educators in similar ways**, stretching our usual practices and prodding us to consider different approaches. The next segment, *Part 4: Working with Breakout Groups,* takes this into account. You can read it in two different ways: 1) to pick up some practices that will help you teach using breakout groups, or 2) to learn about and try out a more group-based model of teaching and learning. You have choices. As a colleague recently explained, "I need a *now-and-later* resource, something that will support me now as I face this shift to teaching live online, and a reference I can consider later when I have more time." At the same time, if you already teach using more collaborative or group-based methods, you'll find Part 4 helpful for adapting your work to the Zoom environment.

The next eight chapters unpack and help us with the second key idea of the book: **Breakout groups are the most important and powerful educational tool in our Zoom toolbox.** But group work doesn't work out-of-the-box. The next chapters help us take a more strategic approach to extended teaching and learning with breakouts. We'll explore what it takes to set up successful learning teams, use etiquette commitments to set expectations, guide their learning with Zoom Preps and discussion guides, and facilitate group learning through the practices of leading, asking, and attending.

WORKING WITH BREAKOUT GROUPS

- Establishing Groups
- Group Etiquette
- Breakout Sizes and Dynamics
- Zoom Preps
- Discussion Guides
- Facilitating Breakouts

GOAL: to strategically form learning teams, guide their work, and facilitate discussion-based and collaborative learning with Zoom breakouts.

Part IV

Working with Breakout Groups

14

ESTABLISHING GROUPS

Teamwork begins by building trust. And the only way to do that is to overcome our need for invulnerability."

— Patrick Lencioni

EARLIER, we reviewed the technical ins and outs of using breakout rooms in Zoom. Now, we move beyond the technical aspects to learn how to set up breakouts for learning. It starts with creating a safe environment for critical thinking. From elementary through graduate settings, I witness educators run right past this important process, regarding team building as a peripheral or perhaps extra-curricular task. I made this mistake for many years because I was operating by an inaccurate notion: I understood critical thinking primarily as an analytical task. However, learning is just as much an emotional process as it is a left-brain activity. **Critical thinking requires us to become vulnerable enough with a group of peers that we become willing to question our long-held assumptions.** Because of this, we cannot take an ad hoc approach to set up breakout groups. Learning groups intended to go beyond short, exploratory activities, will take time and intention to establish. It's a lot like building a good fire.

Building a good fire requires tinder and kindling, spacing the paper and wood so that the oxygen can breathe the fire to life. Similarly, our breakouts require a deliberate 3-step process. We start by establishing *safety*. Second, we invest time and energy building group *cohesion*. Third, we help our students develop the *skills* needed for meaningful discussions and collaborative work.

#1 Establish Safety

Before we get into how to build safety, let's look closer at what it looks like in a small-group setting.

- Safe groups are democratic. No one member dominates the conversation. In a safe group, I'm confident others will listen to one another. In unsafe groups, I'm unsure whether or not my thoughts matter.
- Safe groups have a clearly defined purpose. Unsafe groups feel aimless because expectations are unclear.
- In safe groups, those aspects of myself that make me unique are valued and respected. My ethnic background, gender, previous education, work experience, etc. are seen as advantages to the group. Because of this, my peers are curious to hear my perspective. In unsafe groups, learners overvalue their personal views and fail to appreciate one another.
- In a safe group, I know my instructor will direct the learning without controlling it. And I know that she is willing to intervene if we develop a pattern of going off-track or if our group dynamics deteriorate. In unsafe groups, my instructor is passive.

So, how do we go about building safety? It's tricky because, in the end, each group member must choose to trust their peers. Our job as educators is to create opportunities and to guide the process toward it.

If you want to go fast, go alone. If you want to go far, go together."

—African Proverb

We build safety by providing low-stakes opportunities for our breakout learning teams to get to know one another and take **incremental steps of vulnerability**. These activities must occur early in the life of the group. Our biggest challenge is that these conversations take time and will likely require us to revise our instructional goals, especially during the first several class meetings. However, it's not an all-or-nothing prospect. The best safety-building activities challenge students to integrate the major themes of the course with their personal experiences. I've compiled a set of *8 Group Activities for Building Safety and Trust* that you can download from the *Online Teaching with Zoom webpage* for this chapter.[1]

#2 Build Cohesion

When a learning group develops cohesion, they function more like a team.[2] Teams differ from groups in that they are clear on their purpose. Cohesive learning teams develop a culture with a shared understanding of what is okay and not okay behavior. With a clear purpose and culture, breakout groups acquire a sense of identity that empowers them to move into deeper learning.

The first ingredient for *cohesion* is **consistency**, staying in the same group, and working with the same people. This is why I recommend maintaining group membership for longer terms: for the entire semester, the quarter, or a whole 2-day workshop. Going deep into critical thinking requires what author Kim Scott calls *radical candor*: the ability to care personally and challenge directly.[3] This kind of relationship can only grow when learners meet for frequent and sustained sessions.

To build cohesion, leverage the language of "teams." The term *breakouts* is technically accurate and helpful because it describes *what* they are: breakouts from the main session. However, by referring to our breakout groups as "teams," we move from descriptive language to identity language. Being a *team* means that we have a shared purpose and goal. Our investment goes beyond personal performance because we want the team to win and achieve its collective goal. To make building cohesion more concrete, I've created a resource, *3 Activities for Building Group Cohesion,* that you can download from the *Online Teaching with Zoom webpage* for this chapter.

#3 Develop Group Discussion Skills

Much of our news reporting, political exchange, and social media posting model an unwillingness to listen to others and an entrenched entitlement to our opinions. This can make group discussion a daunting project for educators. Yet, it is also an incredible opportunity to help a generation relearn how to go about constructive dialogue. I'm a firm believer that teachers have a more indelible impact than Instagram influencers and YouTube stars. Recently, my 6th Grade teacher, Mrs. Jones, passed away. She was an expert at matching the right book to the right kid, and from her, I caught my love of reading. It's helpful to recall our impact when we feel like we are spending an inordinate amount of time teaching *how* to have a good conversation. **We are helping our students build skills that will impact all of their relationships for the rest of their lives.** These include the practices of active listening, expressing appreciation, and inquiry.

I've developed an activity called *The Negotiation Exercise* that serves as a skill-building opportunity, and you can access it on the companion webpage to this chapter. However, the best way to help students develop these skills is to assign one skill-development focus or protocol for each activity. To learn the skills of active listening, we can require breakout teams to use a protocol like *The Three Person Rule:* When commenting on another's contribution, each student waits until three group members have spoken before interjecting their response.[4] We might require students to use something similar to Walt Disney's

Plus-It protocol: After each person's initial contribution, comments must add to and build upon the thoughts of others.

What to Do When a Group Becomes Unsafe?

When safety breaks down, it's usually due to an individual in the group who lacks self-awareness or is just unwilling to change their behavior. I'll admit, when teaching high school, my initial response was to change up the groups, moving the "problem child" to a new team. **But groups can build cohesion by successfully navigating conflict.** It just takes an instructor who is willing to intervene and help them work it out. Students need the assurance that we'll be their safety net, available to intervene when they have tried to work things out but arrive at an impasse. As to *how* to work through group problems—well, that's beyond the scope of this book. Two books that I highly recommend are *Never Split the Difference*, by FBI hostage negotiator, Chris Voss, and *Crucial Accountability* by the team over at Vital Smarts. The bottom line is that when we invest early in building group safety, cohesion, and basic discussion skills, we are far less likely to encounter challenging interpersonal issues. Instead of conflict, we establish teams that can learn more together than they could alone.

15

GROUP ETIQUETTE

> I'm not shy about heated debate or passionate discourse,
> but when people get crazy or rude, that's a buzz kill.
> There's got to be a better code of conduct, some basic
> etiquette."
>
> — Mos Def

IN *CHAPTER 10: Classroom Protocols*, we focused on the technology and logistics. I think of these as administrative protocols, basic classroom management. In this chapter, we will concentrate on the *interpersonal* protocols—group etiquette. Our specific recipes for group etiquette will differ depending on the age of our learners, the goals of their learning teams, and our cultural settings. Still, our end goal will be the same regardless of our context: **We want to establish norms of behavior so that our students can conduct vibrant, challenging conversations and work as a team to complete collaborative tasks and projects.**

The Cambridge Dictionary defines etiquette as "the set of rules or customs that control accepted behavior in particular social groups or social situations." Etiquette goes beyond rules. It shapes how we understand *what it means to belong* to a particular group. In other words, etiquette is a powerful tool to shape both accepted behavior and our corporate identity.

Rather than a list of rules, I like to think of these as *commitments* we make to one another. Rules are appropriate, but they tend to focus on negative and individual behavior. While they may need to address some negative behavior, they should point us toward a common positive experience. Instead of prescribing specific rules and behaviors, we can ask our learning teams to create and pledge to follow a set of commitments. These are commitments to such things as mutual respect, self-awareness, and coming prepared to class. These keep us from constantly having to manage group dynamics by placing the responsibility for group cohesion into the hands of our learners. What follows is a set of seven etiquette commitments. You can download this commitment template from the *Online Teaching with Zoom website* and customize them to suit your particular set of students.[1]

Our Commitments (The Etiquette Ingredient List)

Commitment #1: Mutual Respect

Mutual respect is more than a disposition; it must show itself through our actions and words. The key to a good etiquette statement for mutual respect is to make it tangible. Here are a few concrete indicators to describe this commitment to mutual respect.

- We commit to listen to one another and to show that we're listening by asking for more information or clarifications when it would help us to better understand what's been said.
- When we disagree (and we will), we will work to be curious and open.
- We will become more comfortable with silence and allow space for our more reflective peers to think.

- When we disagree or encounter a heated topic, we commit to behave in ways that are not rude or attacking but to have patience with each other during those more challenging moments of conversation.

Commitment #2: Self-Awareness

- We commit to noticing ourselves: our tone, the volume of our voice, our attitude, and to be open to others in the group who point out things we may not be able to notice on our own.
- We commit to notice when we might be slipping into advice-giving and side-conversations.
- We commit to noticing and pointing out when one of us is dominating the conversation and to create more space for other voices.

Commitment #3: A Commitment to Participate

Every learner is a participant, but participation can look very different for different personalities. Consequently, this a commitment that groups should discuss, with each member sharing what they bring to the conversation. An introvert may say, "I'm good at seeing what is missing in a conversation, but it takes me some time to figure it out. So, I'll likely listen for a while and may need some space so that I can speak. It would help if the group could, from time to time, ask me for my thoughts."

The participation commitment is a great place to address the quality of conversation. For example:

- Instead of generic agreements, such as, "I think that's a really good point..." We will respond with specific reasons why or ask specific questions to better understand what's been stated. Here are a couple of examples: "I agree with you, but I'm not exactly sure why. So, it would help me if you would explain more about..." or "That's a good point because it agrees with what Jen was saying about..."

- We commit to staying engaged when there is tension and the topic is stretching us.
- We all take responsibility for moving the conversation forward by asking questions, making connections, and building on the ideas of others.
- We agree to mix things up, not getting stuck in the rut of the same people going in the same order for the same amount of time.

Commitment #4: Paying Attention to Time

This is a shared commitment to progress through the distinct phases of the discussion toward its goal. It may help to designate an individual to do this. If groups choose to have a timekeeper, they should rotate the role within the group.

Commitment #5: To Talk about What's Not Working

This is one of my favorite commitments because it invests everyone in the group with a responsibility to speak up whenever the group finds itself stuck or off-track.

We agree to speak up and talk about the following when we notice them happening:

- When our conversation gets off-topic
- When there is prolonged, unbalanced participation
- When we are stuck and feel like the conversation is going nowhere
- When we are generic or overly agreeable
- When our behavior is not matching our commitments

Commitment #6: Avoid or Decide to Incorporate Side-Conversations

When we notice a side-conversation has developed, we commit to pausing to address it. If it's an important topic and relevant to the group discussion, we will bring it to the group to decide how we might incorporate it into our group conversation. If it is off-topic, we commit to returning our attention to the entire group and the topic at hand.

Commitment #7: Coming Prepared

The quality of our conversation depends on every member coming to class informed and ready. We commit to coming to each class time having completed any Zoom preps, reading, or other assignments needed to have a meaningful conversation or complete our project or task.

Have an Etiquette Discussion

It's tempting to pass out an etiquette checklist, field a few student questions, get their assent, and move on. **But commitment requires a process.** Instead of conducting a brief etiquette overview, devote one of the first group meetings to deliberating these commitments. Here are a few prompts we can use for this purpose:

- What are 1 or 2 commitments most important to you?
- What will be the 1 or 2 most challenging commitments for you?
- How can your group help you with these challenges?
- When you reflect on the entire set of commitments, what's the overall purpose or goal behind them?
- What might you suggest adding to your team's commitments?
- As you reflect on these, what strengths do you bring to the team?

Reinforcing and Modeling Etiquette

For online teachers, regular communication is essential. Usually, this is a weekly email announcement addressing housekeeping items. These announcements provide a perfect opportunity to forecast etiquette that may be pertinent to an upcoming conversation. For instance, a particular discussion may demand more from students' commitment to listening, especially when they disagree. By reminding students of their etiquette commitments, we communicate that these are more than a list of ideals on a sheet of paper only discussed at the beginning of the term.

As mentioned earlier, much of what our students view on television and social media cuts cross-grain to these commitments. Because of this, they need to **see** their teachers model the attributes of constructive discourse. We can do this by hosting embedded conversations within the large-group experience, inviting a set of three to four students to volunteer to participate with the instructor in a challenging conversation "in front of" the larger class.

16

BREAKOUT SIZES AND DYNAMICS

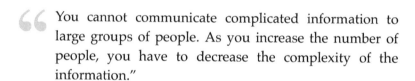 You cannot communicate complicated information to large groups of people. As you increase the number of people, you have to decrease the complexity of the information."

— Andy Stanley

PHYSICAL CLASSROOMS HAVE CONSTRAINTS: square footage, number of chairs, acoustics, whiteboard space, technology limits, lighting controls, etc. If you've taught at a college or university, you've probably experienced the challenges associated with changing classrooms or teaching in multiple classrooms. These spaces we occupy impact learning, and Zoom meetings are no different. To be successful educators, we need to know how the "size" and virtual "space" of the videoconference classroom impacts our students and our learning goals. Let's look at some of these constraints and how we might optimize the sizes of our Zoom classroom.

Group-Sizes

Optimal group size will always depend on our learning goals, the format of the course, and our dominant pedagogy. What follows are a few rules-of-thumb for thinking through group dynamics:

- Large groups benefit from the variety of expertise and experience of the members. However, with more members, participants have fewer opportunities to participate.
- Large groups are suitable for idea generation and shorter conversations.
- Larger groups require a leader to emerge who will direct the conversation. In settings of more than five students, the instructor is typically the group leader.
- Smaller groups benefit from closer relationships, agreement on goals, and more opportunity for participation. They are ideal for completing tasks, projects, and moving deeper into critical thinking.
- Groups of 2-3 work well for peer review and evaluation tasks.
- Groups of 3 tend to be more effective for project-based work.
- Groups of 4 sometimes result in the group breaking into two pairs, and this can mitigate the quality of conversation.
- Groups of 3-5 tend to be optimal for discussion-based learning.

When is a Class or Group Just Too Big for Discussion?

When you combine the realities of screen real estate and group dynamics, we hit the ceiling for academic discussions around 10-12 learners. For conversations to move further into critical thinking, we probably hit that ceiling at 5-6 learners. After these inflection points, we need to adapt by leveraging breakout rooms for more in-depth learning conversations, and strategically using large-group session structures for things like debriefs and presenting new material.

Should I Choose Groups or Allow Students to Choose?

Choose groups for your students at random. This allows your groups to develop their own identity and style of relating. It also makes room for a more diverse learning team. When students self-select groups, they choose peers they know and like, and those relationships come with a set of built-in relational dynamics that tend to stifle good learning conversations. This, of course, is not always the case, but it is the strong tendency of self-selected groups. Most learning management systems will generate course groups randomly and by the desired group size. This is the best way to establish groups because it then allows you to communicate with your groups via the LMS. It also sets you up to offer asynchronous discussions and other online activities by groups within your Learning Management System. Additionally, there are random group generators available online (just search for *random group generators*).

Large Group Limitations

In large groups (more than 12), communication will tend toward monologue rather than dialogue and information-sharing rather than higher-order thinking activities like problem-solving. We must face these facts so that we don't find them working against us. For most students, large-group discussion is spectator dialogue because they spend most of their time observing, rather than participating in, the conversation. However, interviews can make for fascinating spectator dialogue. Invite a colleague, practitioner, or subject matter expert to a class session. Involve your students by having them submit questions or participate in a time of Q&A.

Technical Limitations

We could conceivably include thousands of students in our Zoom classroom.[1] However, if you want to see your students and interact with them individually, the four walls of the live video session are the four sides of your screen. As teachers, this will be our most obvious limitation because it impacts how many students you can see and interact with while you teach. Right now, Zoom can accommodate up to 49 participants on one screen in its *gallery view*. This can be further limited by the capacity of your computer's processor and whether or not you have the most up-to-date Zoom software. These more technical realities are essential to consider as we think through what we expect to work and won't work in this space.

In the next two chapters, we're going to shift gears from team building to *team guiding*. We'll do this by providing our learning teams with two essential tools: Zoom Preps and discussion guides.

17

ZOOM PREPS

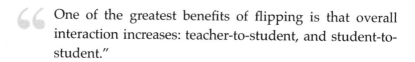 One of the greatest benefits of flipping is that overall interaction increases: teacher-to-student, and student-to-student."

— Aaron Sams, *Flip Your Classroom*

I HAVE the joy of working with an incredible team of instructional designers. One of our instructional designers was working with a professor to develop a new online course that included several Zoom class sessions. But the first live session fell flat. Conversation limped along, and the professor felt too much responsibility to carry the work of learning. The instructional designer immediately recognized the problem, so she asked, "Did you require a Zoom Prep before the session?" The idea hadn't occurred to him. So, they set to work crafting a brief preparation activity for each of his future Zoom meetings. The next week, the professor dropped by our office to share that his student conversations turned the corner and improved significantly.

When we design Zoom sessions, the most important question we can ask ourselves is: **How will my students prepare for this meeting?** This kind of pre-work will radically improve the quality of discussion and collaboration. At the same time, I'm not a fan of adding a bunch of extra work for students. Over the days and weeks of a course, this can compound into a burden and start to feel like busywork. Two principles can keep us out of this ditch and make these activities meaningful.

#1 - Keep Zoom Prep exercises brief

#2 - Keep Zoom Preps meaningful by integrating them with existing work, such as assigned reading, lecture viewing, or other more significant assignments.

Let's look at a couple examples to get a sense of how Zoom Preps work.

Zoom Prep Instructions and Examples

Example #1

Preparing for our Zoom Session: This week, take notes while viewing the lecture videos. Jot down 2-3 questions you have about the material. Afterward, spend 5-10 minutes reviewing your notes and reflecting. Allow space for other questions to emerge. Use this time to select one question you would like to pose to the class during our Zoom session. Post this question in this week's online forum by Wednesday at 11:55 PM. I will review these before our time together, and we'll discuss them in class.

Let's dissect this example and draw out a few tips from it.

1. Be Specific. The example asks students for 2-3 questions, then to narrow to one question for posting.

2. Focus Attention. Our students get saturated with information. Our Zoom Prep instructions should help them focus on what matters most for the upcoming session. Is it a chapter in their reading, a specific article, or a segment of a video? Direct their attention to what matters most and what you plan to discuss in your live session.

3. Concrete Action. The best prep exercises include a means of accountability by requiring students to take a simple and concrete action. In our example, students post a question before the session, and by a specific day and time.

4. Use Minutes. Without a time-boundary, the type-A, perfectionist students can pour hours into a brief prep exercise. Other students will not invest enough time and attention to the work. The solution is to time-box the activity. Our example asks the students to spend 5-10 minutes, reflecting on their notes and choosing a question.

5. Your Follow-up. Explain how you will use their prep work in the session. This integration creates accountability and removes it from the category of busywork.

6. Supports Existing Work. This preparation exercise supports the existing work of asynchronous lecture viewing instead of adding a completely different and new task.

Example #2

Here's a second example that leverages an existing project and a collaborative session structure.

By Monday, you will have completed the first draft of your paper. Before our session, invest about 15 minutes reading over your paper to determine what feedback you need. At the top of your paper, type out 2-3 requests for feedback. Have this ready to screen share in your breakout groups during this week's live session.

To Grade or Not to Grade

Our grading philosophy will determine how we approach Zoom Preps. First, I want to get a good estimate for *how much time* I'm requiring my students to invest in prep work. If I'm asking for a significant investment, then I might want to consider making these a graded element of the course. At the same time, we don't want to proliferate graded items in our courses (online courses are infamous for this—much to the chagrin of teachers and students alike). One solution to this is to create a one-question completion quiz each week where students indicate whether or not they have completed their Zoom Prep prior to class. Because these are non-qualitative and self-reported measures, I might give Zoom Preps a smaller weight in the overall grading structure. Even with a low weighting, students tend to take these graded items more seriously than a non-graded item.

Another helpful solution is to use a more detailed self-assessment. In these, students reflect on their Zoom Prep work, their consistency in doing them before class, how prepared they feel for the conversations, and how they can improve their contribution to future discussions. I like this approach because it's a meta-cognitive task. The self-assessment approach also reinforces the sense of responsibility each learner has for the quality of their team discussions. To implement this approach, provide students with a short rubric and an online quiz or assignment submission where they can post their responses. These online submissions also serve as a great place to provide students with feedback. For instance, a student may self-report that they are doing a great job in coming prepared for the conversation. Still, I may have noticed a couple of sessions where it was evident that they had rushed through or not fully completed the Zoom Prep. Such situations provide me an opportunity to note the discrepancy and suggest ways for my students to improve.

 We should remember that good fortune often happens when opportunity meets with preparation."

— Thomas A. Edison

Make Zoom Preps Meaningful Work

As teachers, we can see how a Zoom Prep meets our learning objectives, but our students must be able to see and feel the connection. Unless Zoom Preps are integrated into the life of the course, students will see them as unnecessary and obligatory elements. Here are three tips for integrating Zoom Preps into your course so that they don't become disconnected extras.

#1 Scaffold larger assignments

Typically, our courses require students to place a disproportionate amount of time, effort, and concern into a final project or two or three larger assignments. How can their Zoom Prep and conversations scaffold these projects and papers? If it's a good assignment, then it's worthy of this kind of time and discussion. Look through your major assignments and make a list of topics or ideas that directly relate to what students must understand to complete their work. Finally, explain the linkage to students. Make it explicit by writing out, "This Zoom Prep and our conversation this week will help you think through a couple of key parts of your final paper..."

#2 Make it true Zoom Prep or throw it out

Students should feel like the prep is an essential element and not additional or unrelated work. The primary culprit for this—at least that I've witnessed—is unused preps. For example, students spend time reading an article, watching videos, responding to questions. Still, the teacher never gets to the topic of the prep in class. I've been guilty of this, particularly in over-prepare-mode, when I have more material than I can reasonably work through in a class session. At best, students are disappointed. At worst, students resent the prep work and stop investing time in them. As we'll see in the chapter on discussion guides, it's helpful to note the dependencies between Zoom Preps and discussion guides. **Creating explicit links between the preps and discussion guides is probably the best habit I can think of for keeping things integrated.** It also prevents us from unintentionally disregarding the work students have done to prepare for class.

#3 Set them up for failure

Okay, I realize that we never want to really set our students up for failure. But I thought that might get your attention. What I mean here is we make the Zoom Prep so essential to the upcoming conversation, that to come unprepared makes the conversation or task so challenging that students quickly learn the importance of these activities. This is especially helpful during the early weeks of a course because it communicates to our students that we are serious about the prep work.

Delivering Zoom Prep Instructions

Finally, there are several ways we can deliver the instructions for our prep exercises.

- Build a dedicated space on your online course site to house them.
- Create an appendix to your syllabus listing all the prep exercises.
- Send Zoom Preps via class announcements or email.

The first two approaches allow for editing, but they communicate a more static sequence to the course. If your teaching style is more adaptive and you want to customize your prep for each session, you can send out the prep exercise instructions as a class-wide announcement. Just be sure you are consistent in sending these out well ahead of time so that your learners have enough time to complete them before class.

18

DISCUSSION GUIDES

> " I want to…[stress] how important it is that small group activities be carefully structured. The activities students say they find to be most productive are the ones in which the ground rules are clearly stated and understood."

> - Stephen Brookfield, *Teaching for Critical Thinking*

ANOTHER WAY TO create structure in the Zoom classroom is to provide our breakout teams with discussion or activity guides. These give our learning teams a step-by-step process for their conversation or collaborative task. Additionally, they help teams focus on the learning objective, point out the necessary skills, and reference the etiquette commitments most relevant to their work. In what follows, we'll review the essential elements of an effective discussion or activity guide. (For guide examples, see the companion webpage for this chapter.)[1]

A Basic Outline for Discussion Guides

1. A Scenario, Case, Common Reading, Simulation, Problem Statement, or Task

This is the setup and the heart of the discussion or activity. Here we define the objective, pose the problem, and describe the task.

2. Necessary Resources

What prior learning or common understanding do students need to succeed in this activity? This is where our Zoom Preps will often integrate into these guides. Addressing the Zoom Prep directly within the discussion guides creates a sense of social accountability and a positive peer pressure to come to the group prepared. Usually, the initial prompt or phase of the activity or discussion is to review the Zoom Prep. In addition to the Zoom Prep, other necessary resources may include a short article pdf, a web link to a resource, textbook page references, or course notes.

3. Framework

The framework outlines for your breakout teams the specific steps they must take to move through to accomplish their work. One of the teacher-side benefits of this outline is that it will help you see where your learning teams are most likely to need your support. You'll know when to jump in and clarify things, offer new lines of inquiry, or challenge them to persist during the more difficult phases of their work.

4. Etiquette Commitments

Here we call on our etiquette commitments and forecast how specific commitments may apply to the conversation at hand.

5. Necessary Skills

Think of a specific discussion or collaboration skill you want your students to practice or is essential to the success of their work. Then build it into your guide. Such skills include: pausing to reflect, appreciation, asking follow-up questions, active-listening practices, the delegation of tasks, debriefing prior project work, understanding checks, summarizing the thoughts of others, etc.

6. Keep it Simple

I recommend keeping discussion guides to a half-page in length. Any more than that and you're likely bogging the team down with too much detail. We are aiming for *just enough* structure to scaffold their time and not so much that we inadvertently stifle conversations or micromanage their tasks. However, if you have a class that meets more than once a week, consider structuring the entire week with an extended discussion guide.

7. Timeboxing

Provide timeboxes for the different phases of the conversation. For example, students might spend 15 minutes discussing a case or scenario, clarifying the problem, and level setting common understandings. In phase two, they spend 20 minutes examining the evidence, and in phase three, they spend five minutes creating a summary to share with the large group. By creating these milestones, you'll keep breakout teams moving at a similar pace and make your job supporting them much easier.

19

FACILITATING BREAKOUTS

EARLIER, I mentioned that Part 4 has both are *now* and *later* segments. This chapter on facilitating breakouts probably falls into that *later* category. You won't necessarily need these skills to get started teaching with Zoom, but they will help you later to improve your teaching. There are three core skills to facilitate learning in breakout groups: 1) assertive leadership, 2) asking questions, and 3) attending to the subtext of conversations and group dynamics.

Facilitating Breakouts

✓ Leading

Asking Questions

Attending

Assertive Leadership

Students want their learning experience to flow, to feel dynamic, marked by back-and-forth and give-and-take. They loathe the awkward pauses, and get thrown off by classrooms where the communication feels hesitant and uncertain. Actually, there are technical reasons for why the videoconference classroom is prone to this awkwardness.[1] The principal reason is latency. Latency is the gap between when the person speaks and when it's heard. You can test this and experience it by opening a Zoom meeting. Now, stare at yourself. Then blink. You'll see yourself blink—*after* you've blinked! This lag in communication makes the videoconferenced classroom prone to a stutter-step experience and clumsy communication. **The primary solution for latency is to become more assertive in how we lead our students.** The following eight skills are helpful for leading breakout groups, and many of the principles transferrable to large-group and in-person settings.

The Skills of Assertive Leadership

#1 Interrupting

I'm a peacemaker at heart, so I hate interrupting my students. By interrupting, many of us fear we will communicate a lack of respect or devalue our students' contributions. In the Zoom classroom, strategic interrupting (or we could call it "interjecting") helps us overcome the hesitancy that latency tends to generate.

 One of the issues I kept saying to my students is you have to learn to interrupt. When you raise your hand at a meeting, by the time they get to you, the point is not germane. So the bottom line is active listening. If you are going to interrupt, you look for opportunities. You have to know what you are talking about."

— Madeleine Albright

As Madeleine Albright explains in the above quote, we can respectfully interrupt, but to do so demands a high level of attention. This is another reason why the Zoom classroom can be so mentally and physically demanding.

The best tool for this is to use an interruption phrase that best fits your personality and teaching style. Here are a few to consider:

- Address the student by name and summarize, "Trent, what I hear you saying is…"
- Address the student by name and give attention to something important they said, "Amanda, I want to point out something you said…"
- You'll notice the first two approaches both lead with the student's name. It's the most powerful single word you can use to turn the conversation. Sometimes the best thing to do is say their name and pause for them to respond with a "yes." They have now given you the floor.
- "Let's just pause for just a second."
- Interrupt with a screen share. Let your students know that you may, at times, overtake the screen. Normalize this by telling students what to do when this happens. "When we are in conversation, and I share a slide, I want you to know that I value what you're saying. At the same time, I want to transition the conversation. When this happens, try to wrap up your thoughts in 30 seconds or less."

We can also interrupt with our body language. Move closer to the camera to signal to the student that it's time to conclude their thoughts. If we make this cue a consistent habit, many of our learners will recognize it as a dependable signal that we are ready for them to wrap up.

Normalize interruption by talking with your students about how and why you will interrupt. You might say something like, "I'm going to interrupt every one of you this semester. Often, it's because you've said something important, and I wanted to slow down the conversation and give that point particular attention. At other times, the conversation may have diverged too far from our original learning goal, so I'll bring us back on track. But I want you to be confident that I never intend to disrespect you or your ideas."

#2 Pacing

We have a phenomenon up in the high country of the Rocky Mountains called *flash-boom-flash lightning*. Bolts of lightning rain down in such succession that the next bolt hits while you are still hearing and feeling the thunder produced by the prior strike. Good conversations have a flash-boom-flash dynamic. Observe any discussion you have today and notice how quickly the responses occur and even overlap one another. Because these interchanges occur in fractions-of-a-second, the latency of videoconferencing just can't keep up. Because of this, we have to slow down our conversations. While this can feel frustrating, it may be just what we need to become more reflective teachers and learners. When we slow down, we listen better, we become more thoughtful, and perhaps more patient with one another. We'll explore this more in the practice of attending.

#3 Normalizing Silence

Not all gaps in conversation are bad. Brookfield and Preskill encourage us to see silence as normal and helpful: "Don't panic at silence. At the start of a discussion, there may be long periods of silence as people settle into the new intellectual project that the conversation represents."[2] To make our students comfortable with silence, we first have to be okay with it ourselves. I find that a subtle smile during those periods of quiet, taking the time to jot down notes on a piece of paper, even looking up and to the right as I ponder, tell my students that we are in a non-anxious space.

 Don't mistake students' silence for mental inertia or disengagement. Conversation is halting, tentative, and circuitous, filled with hesitations and awkward attempts at reformulating thoughts even as we speak them."

— Brookfield and Preskill in *Discussion as a Way of Teaching*.

In addition to modeling silence in the conversation, we can explain how quiet spaces contribute to our learning by providing us time to reflect and observe. Talk with students about those awkward moments when the conversation stalls. Instead of seeing them as uncomfortable threats, reframe them as important transition points where we can stay in the silence and reflect, ask for an understanding check, or regroup the conversation.

#4 Creating Equity

Students tell us they desire everyone to speak up and share during a discussion, and for each person to speak for an equal amount of time. This is an idealized expectation. The heart of this desire is good, but the only way to guarantee this kind of 100% equality in conversation is to impose policies that are more likely to stifle it. Moreover, introverted learners and internal processors may not desire equal talk time. Often, a 10-second contribution by a reflective student provides disproportionate value, changing and deepening the course of the conversation. So, what is at the heart of students' desire for equal time to talk? I think it's a sense of equity.

We'll define equity as all students knowing they have the same opportunity to contribute to the conversation, and that everyone in the class or group will respect their contributions. Equity is established, not in one conversation, but within the group culture throughout many discussions or breakout collaborations. Instead of equity, we might have them consider balance or fairness—whatever term best suits our setting. But many of our learners will likely have to move from their idealized expectations of "equal time" to the "equal opportunity and respect" mindset. An effective way to lead students into this mindset is with moments of brief reflection, situated near the end of class. For example:

- What made your conversation feel balanced, or perhaps out of balance?
- As you look toward to future team discussions (or tasks), what would help you strike a balance of participation?

Much of how we create equity comes down to how we work with dominant voices and quieter students. It's an art, but one we can learn and develop.

#5 Working with Dominant Voices

Dominant voices can create a myriad of problems and significantly disrupt learning for a majority of students. Outspoken students, when allowed to command the conversation, often reinforce a single perspective. Additionally, their peers might perceive them as authoritative or privileged. This perception can further isolate already marginalized voices. In the worst cases, if we leave dominant voices unchecked, quieter students feel alienated and resolve to keep silent. Our goal is not to silence or even manage these voices but to create an equitable and balanced classroom experience. The following practices will aid us as we seek to do so.

Communicate your goals. By communicating our classroom goals early in the class, we set expectations, and we cast a vision that we can return to throughout term. In her excellent article, "Teaching Strategies for Classroom Equity," Dr. Kimberly Tanner explains, "Perhaps the most powerful teaching strategy in building an inclusive and equitable learning environment is for instructors to be explicit that the triad of access, fairness, and classroom equity is one of their key goals."[3] These values and goals become more meaningful when we can explain to our students how they support learning, create a culture of diverse perspectives, and shape an environment of openness.

Encourage self-awareness. Generally, the real problem with dominant speakers is not a lack of self-control but a lack of self-awareness. We can pull these students aside by contacting them via email or a private message in the Zoom chat to set up a meeting to discuss their tendency to talk. Talk about the unintended consequences of speaking too often, and how it might be impacting the rest of the class. Encourage them to slow down and build their reflection skills. Many of these students have a deep need to be heard. Spend some time getting to know them, their life situation, and their goals. End the meeting with a clear and simple plan, then ask them to type it out and send you a copy via email. The email makes the commitment official and becomes something you can reference in the future, both to remind them of their commitment and to celebrate their progress.

Give dominant voices a role. A friend was attempting to train a young German shepherd that was incredibly intelligent but unruly. He scheduled an appointment with a professional trainer. The trainer observed the dog, walked to his trunk, pulled out a dog backpack, and fastened the harness straps around the animal. "He's a working breed of dog. He needs a job." The dog's behavior immediately shifted, and my friend was able to work with him.

It's kind of weird to compare a student to a dog. My intent instead is to focus on the principle. I was this kind of student in school. I was stir-crazy unless I had something to do (I'm still this way). Many of our more vocal students fall into this category and would benefit from having an active role within their learning team or the large group. Such tasks might include taking notes, creating an outline, developing slides, managing a collaborative document, group facilitator, question asker, fact-checker, small-group presenter, or consensus builder. A well-defined role is more likely to be well-executed. And in small groups, it's especially helpful to rotate these roles.

#6 Drawing out the Quiet Students

There is a myriad of reasons why students may be unwilling or feel uncomfortable to talk, especially in a large-group setting. Without one-on-one conversations with each of them, it's impossible to discern. However, there are a couple of go-to practices that have a disproportionately positive impact on more introverted learners: **creating safety and creating spaces for reflection.** We've touched on these practices, and here we'll look more specifically at how we can leverage these to support our more reserved students.

Creating safety. While writing this book, I observed an evening graduate course where the professor did a masterful job of creating a welcoming and safe setting. He included everyone by name, was genuinely interested in each of them, but he did one thing that stood out: *He was vulnerable.* At multiple points in the class session, he shared his own mistakes and shortcomings as both a teacher and a professional. He could have said, "There are no stupid questions in my class," and that would have been fine. However, he went further and modeled it for his students. His sharing communicated, "I don't have it all together. *We* don't have it all together. And I don't expect *you* to have it all together in my classroom." Such words persuade our more introverted learners that it's safe to speak and share in our classrooms.

 Quiet thinkers are often motivated to speak more by seeing how their voices shift the conversation."

— Kara Pranikoff, *Teaching Talk*

The most profound and conversation shifting comments often come from my more introverted learners. They are much more at home with silence than their extroverted peers, and they value an instructor who is comfortable with moments of quiet. When the teacher becomes comfortable, she can set the entire virtual room at ease, endorsing and valuing the introvert's more composed disposition.

Creating spaces for reflection. A simple but effective practice is to take a few 30-second pauses during our sessions. We can only normalize these silent, reflective spaces when we model it through practice. Another way to introduce silence and reflection into our classrooms is by making it active with an online reflection activity. Google forms are perhaps the easiest and most accessible way to create these. Alternatively, we can build these using essay type quiz questions or survey modules within our LMS. Kara Pranikoff, in her excellent book *Teaching Talk,* calls this act of quiet reflection *lingering.* She explains, "We want students to linger in their thinking, to allow themselves the time and space to sit with an idea, to understand that brilliance does not come in a flash, and that thinking takes time."[4]

Another alternative is to give our quieter learners permission to reflect and share their ideas in the chat. We can reference these, read them out loud for the class, and ask students to expound about the ideas they have posted. For example, "Libby, in the chat, you mentioned a theory that I believe we overlooked in our earlier conversation. Do you feel comfortable explaining how you think it may apply to the topic at hand?"

Did you notice I gave Libby an out? Introverted learners like to know they have an option. Giving them a safe place often means giving them both the opportunity to talk and the opportunity to decline. More often than not, they will choose to share.

#7 Calling on Students (Raising Hands)

I've recommended a more open and reflexive Zoom classroom, one with unmuted microphones where students are encouraged to jump into the conversation. However, this may not be realistic in your context. In this case, raising hands is a time-proven solution, but Zoom presents some challenges. With over twenty students on the screen—even with a large monitor—it can be difficult to notice raised hands. And the *raise hand* feature in Zoom's participants list is difficult to see and cumbersome to use. We need something that makes a raised hand more prominent. A white index card or folded sheet of paper does the trick. It's a much more apparent and visual signal because of the movement it produces when a student raises the paper in front of their camera. The new *reactions* feature in Zoom is a lot easier to see than the tiny *raised hand* indicator because the reactions (clapping hands and thumbs up icons) are larger and appear within the student thumbnails. You just have to redefine their use and ask your students to use them to signal a raised hand.

#8 *Managing the Clock.* Working with breakout groups requires a higher level of time-management. I've found that it helps to **communicate in the language of minutes and clock-time**. There is a big difference between when a teacher says, "We are going to take a 10-minute break," and when they say, "We are going to take a 10-minute break *and be back in here and ready to go at 11:45.*" The more we can be explicit about time, the more likely we are to arrive on time. Being this precise may initially feel like micromanagement, but the practice goes a long way to replace some of the boundaries and borders that we often lose in the virtual classroom.

Facilitating Breakouts

Leading

✓ Asking Questions

Attending

Asking Questions

The quality of our questions makes the difference between an engaging learning experience and a humdrum activity. This difference is usually surgical, requiring us to fine-tune just a few words. Take this common question as an example; one we often pose after a presentation or lecture:

"Does anyone have questions?"

What's wrong with this question? Expert interviewers would immediately notice that this is a *closed question*, a question that elicits a yes or no answer. It boxes the learner into binary thinking, which undermines open inquiry. Now, let's make our surgical tweak.

"What questions do you have?"

This surgically tuned question is open. It assumes that inquiry is taking place, that the learners have questions, and it may even assume that we, as the teachers, have been unclear or perhaps have overlooked important information. Let's look further into the characteristics of a good question.

Some Characteristics of a Good Question

- They are open, not binary, and therefore keep students open to inquiry.
- They lead learners to be concrete and specific with their responses.
- They directly support your learning objectives.
- Good questions address cognitive domains when the goal is cognitive (e.g., to analyze a problem or to apply a new concept).
- They address affective domains when dealing with affective goals and values (e.g., asking for emotional responses, concerns, etc.).

- Good questions recognize students' zone of proximal development and scaffold inquiry into the next level of critical thinking.[5]

Beginning, Middle, and End

Most discussions require us to spend 10% of the time to get the ball rolling, about 80% of the time in the heart of the conversation, and 10% wrapping things up. Each segment has unique goals, so let's consider questions that help in each of these three phases of learning conversations.

Questions for Beginning a Discussion

I have a 1987 Toyota 4Runner. At the time of this writing, it's 32 years old and has over 350K miles on it. A few years ago, I took it to a mechanic to have him look it over, and he gave me one vital tip: When it's cold outside, take some time to let it warm up. By starting the engine and giving the truck a few minutes to warm up, the engine performs better when under the stress of driving. A cold start is hard for students, too. Because of this, **the best question to begin a discussion is the question students have considered *before* coming to class.** You guessed it: Zoom Prep questions are the best place to start. These questions set the context for the conversation and are often exploratory. We are not yet going deep but setting the stage. Here are a few examples:

- "After having finished the reading, how would you sum up what you learned in one to two sentences?"
- "As you view the online lecture material before class, I'd like to consider one big question…Write out a brief 3-4 sentence reflection on the question and come to class prepared to discuss this."
- "What's the most important finding or piece of evidence from your reading?"

These questions create anchor points and context for the larger conversation.

Another approach is to give our students the question at the beginning of class and provide them a few minutes to reflect and write. When we do this, however, we should clearly communicate the goal. Is it to set up a conversation, or is it to set up a lecture? When we ask a question, students assume a conversation. We can unintentionally bait and switch our students if we regularly ask prep questions only to tee-up a lecture segment. This isn't a bad technique; it's just important that we set the expectation so that our students understand the purpose of their inquiry.

We can also start class with an exploratory question. Michael Stanier, in his excellent book, *The Coaching Habit,* recommends beginning conversations with the question, "What's on your mind?"[6] It may seem a bit dangerous to be so open-ended. But the value in such a question is the vast array of potential responses. Students may explain how they are thinking about the topic or how distracted they are with worry over the upcoming exam or assignment. It's a learner-centered question that can give us a pulse on our students as we begin class.

 It is not that I'm so smart. But I stay with the questions much longer."

- Albert Einstein

Questions for the Middle of a Discussion

The middle is where we spend most of our conversation. The questions we ask here depend upon our learning goals. If these goals are *cognitive,* we may want to move students from a basic understanding of a concept to the application in a real-world case. If our goal is *affective,* we need questions that get students to consider their values, how they feel about an idea, what they believe about it, etc. With adult learners, we will want to ask questions like, "How do you see this working or not working in *your* professional setting?" Some of the most valuable questions are about the conversation itself, metacognitive questions like, "Are we off track?" or "We have just 20 minutes left. So, what direction should we take?" At the companion webpage for this chapter, you'll find question prompts and stems to use for a variety of learning goals.[7]

Questions for Concluding a Discussion

Our brains have an insatiable need to close the loop. We must see the end of the movie, or the scene, hear the final note resolve in the music, finish the chapter or paragraph, or sentence we are reading. It's the same in our conversations. We need some questions to tie things up and consolidate our thoughts.

- We have about five minutes left. What do we need to remember when we pick up this conversation again next week?
- What did we accomplish today in our conversation?
- What is the most memorable thing you'll take away from this conversation?
- If you had to choose right now, with the information you've gained, what would your group decide?
- What is unresolved that you would like to better understand or talk about the next time we meet? Why?
- What did your group discover or conclude that you believe would be helpful to the entire class?

Some Final Tips for Asking Questions

Tip #1 - Use questions that begin with "What" instead of "Why." Questions that begin with "What" are particularly helpful when asking students to provide evidence or to justify their point of view. For example, we can transform, "Why did you come to that conclusion?" to "What led you to that conclusion?" The *why question* can unnecessarily put some students on the defensive, while the *what question* assumes the student has clear reasons, even when they have yet to process or explain them.

Tip #2 - Lead with curiosity. Start questions with phrases like, "That's interesting..." "Now, you have us curious..." "I think you've got us wondering..." These stems cultivate openness and go a long way to reinforce to students that this is a safe environment for their thoughts to grow through discussion.

Tip #3 - Soften questions with "perhaps..." I like the word "perhaps" because it keeps us from leading the witness. Some more direct questions can feel like an accusation, or that a teacher is assuming things about me. "Perhaps" keeps the door open and promotes possibility thinking. For example, instead of saying, "How is this concept confronting our stereotypes and biases?" we might say, "Perhaps this concept is confronting some of our stereotypes and biases. (Pause) Would one of you be willing to reflect on this for us?"

Facilitating Breakouts

Leading

Asking Questions

✓ Attending

Attending

Attending is the practice of observing, then engaging students from that place of having observed. It is sometimes called *active listening*. While attending, we notice the beliefs of our students they may not be aware of, the tensions between students, the force they use to communicate—in short, we are paying attention to the **subtext** of the conversation, the human elements. Attending is challenging because, to observe, I first must set aside what I want to say. The task is made even more complicated because our role as teachers has been defined as *telling*. The very terms we use for our profession are *teacher, professor,* and *instructor*. All of those describe a *telling* role. Consequently, to observe and notice can feel passive. However, attending is an incredibly demanding practice.

 It's worth acknowledging the amount of mental energy it takes just to listen and think within a conversation."

Kara Pranikoff, *Teaching Talk*

To What Are We Attending?

- **Assumptions:** The tacit beliefs our students hold that can disappear into the background of their conversations.
- **Level of energy and emotion:** Energy and emotion show up in our tone. We communicate them through body language and the volume of our voice. Often, speakers are not aware of the level of energy they are bringing to a conversation.
- **How connected the speaker to others.** Is the speaker overly detached or self-protective? Perhaps they are merged with the group and having a difficult time differentiating so that they can know and share their point of view.
- **Interpersonal dynamics:** Is there relational tension getting in the way of meaningful conversation? Left unaddressed, interpersonal dynamics can overwhelm a conversation.
- **Avoiding Ownership:** We feel safe when we can keep an idea

at a distance. Most of the time, this dynamic is subtle, but we see this come up in learning conversations as students avoid owning their beliefs and emotions. A lack of ownership is evident when we speak about the positions of others but never address our own perspective, talking about "them" and "us" instead of "me" and "my." We also sidestep ownership by speaking in abstractions and generalizations. We can avoid ownership by creating the never-ending-list of problems, avoiding the crux of a matter by hiding it among a litany of other issues or details. As you attend, you'll be amazed at the creative ways we humans use to avoid dealing with the most critical problems and uncomfortable ideas we encounter.

- **Specific emotions:** We attend to the unspoken feelings playing out in the conversation, coming from individuals or being experienced by the group.
- **Connections:** Brookfield and Preskill say, "...one of the most valuable benefits of good listening is that it increases continuity."[8] As we attend, we notice the common threads, themes, or how a recent comment relates to something another student said ten minutes ago. By making connections, we can create a more cohesive experience between learners and between concepts.

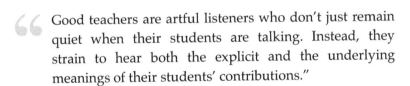

Good teachers are artful listeners who don't just remain quiet when their students are talking. Instead, they strain to hear both the explicit and the underlying meanings of their students' contributions."

— Brookfield and Preskill, *Discussion as a Way of Teaching*

What to Do with What We Have Observed?

- We share with the group what we've noticed. "I want to pause us for just a moment because I've noticed..."
- We speak directly to specific students, "John, I noticed that when we start talking about _____ you lean forward like you have something you want to say." "Jasmine, you've been quiet

for much of our conversation, but I noticed you shaking your head in disagreement with something earlier. Would you be willing to share?"

- Speak to group dynamics: "While we were talking, I noticed something. We seem to be talking *around* and not directly about the part racism may have to play in this. Why do you think we are responding this way?"

Attending Requires Time

It's difficult, maybe impossible, to drop into breakout groups for a few minutes and attend to the conversation. Without the context of the prior conversation, we may pull things out of context. The group may perceive us as an outsider. To attend, we must be present for longer durations of time, preferably from the beginning of the conversation. If we drop into it after it's started, then it's a good idea to ask the group to catch us up on the progress of the conversation. Depending on the duration of our class, it means we may only get to one or two breakout groups during the session. In that case, we should let our students know how we plan to rotate between groups and how often.

Because attending is an art, anticipate failing a good bit as you try it out. Don't worry; any lack of success is not proof that it doesn't work. It's just proof we need more practice. It's a practice that will benefit us in the classroom, in our professional and our personal relationships.

Part V

Wrapping Up

20

IMPROVING OUR GAME

"One of the biggest myths about self-awareness is that it's all about looking inward—that is, insight from the inside out. But armed with only our own observations, even the most dedicated students of self-awareness among us risk missing a key piece of the puzzle."

— Tasha Eurich, *Insight*

ANDERS ERICSSON, researcher and professor of psychology, studied how experts went from having ordinary skills to becoming expert performers. His research found that experts followed a similar approach to improve their skills, one that he terms *deliberate practice*. The critical component to deliberate practice was **feedback**. Experts became experts because they elicited feedback, then worked that feedback into their practice.

Asking for and listening to feedback is incredibly challenging. I would rather get everything right the first time. I don't want people pointing out my weaknesses, and I don't enjoy reflecting on my mistakes. We invest a lot of energy avoiding those things. But if we can negotiate that emotional barrier and work feedback into our practice, it's what will make the difference between plateauing at the level of a good teacher or pressing on to become a master teacher.

Zoom provides us a unique opportunity to transform our teaching and improve our craft like never before. We can collect and review feedback from polls, chats, and recordings to become more responsive, find our blind spots, and even improve our teaching skills in-the-moment. The technology puts this all within our reach—if we have the courage to ask for and listen to the feedback.

Feedback offers us another way to build rapport with our students. When students see us work their feedback into our teaching, we engender trust and respect. Further, when we ask for feedback, we model for our students what it looks like to be curious, lifelong learners. Many students get stuck in their learning because they believe they have to get it right all the time. When we model this openness to critique, we chip away at the fear of failure that prevents so many students from overcoming this barrier to learning.

Feedback also gives us a more accurate understanding of our students' learning needs. We hear a lot of talk about differentiated instruction and matching our teaching to a variety of learning needs. Feedback is what clues us in on those needs in a more personized way. *Personized* is a term coined by professor of organizational psychology, Ed Schein.[1] It may be best understood by comparing the idea with the more familiar concept of *personalizing*. We *personalize* education when we customize our teaching to the needs of an individual. *Personizing* is less about customization and more about **connection and relationship**. From a student perspective, it's the sense that you understand how I think and what I value. I trust you because you are the type of person who hears and understands me. Our responsiveness to feedback makes that possible.

Zoom offers us an unprecedented set of opportunities to make feedback a regular part of our teaching. What follows are six methods and tips for implementing feedback in your virtual classroom.

#1 Record and Watch Yourself

It's not thrilling to go back and view ourselves teaching, but evidence shows it may be *the most effective way* to improve our craft. For over 15 years, the Melbourne Educational Research Institute has conducted a project to synthesize over 800 meta-analyses to find out what practices most impact student achievement.[2] Toward the very top of the list of over 200 indicators is a practice called **microteaching**. Microteaching includes recording a brief teaching session, then sitting down to review the recording with a fellow teacher, supervisor, or a community of practice.

In the past, this required expensive equipment and was time-consuming. With Zoom, these recording tools are right at your fingertips. Instead of a video camera on a tripod at the back of the classroom, Zoom has a live camera on the teacher and every student, recording our responses and facial expressions. Zoom also creates transcripts of the session by converting speech to text, providing you with a valuable verbatim document (this transcription is not always accurate, and it's sometimes humorous, but it's still helpful).

You can automate this by setting your Zoom account to record every session automatically. The key to this practice is to team up with at least one other colleague to get outside feedback. This also gives you an opportunity to learn from their recorded sessions. Keep the reviews short, watching segments of your instruction. (See the companion webpage for this chapter for more resources on microteaching).[3]

#2 Use Polls for Informal Checks

As an online course developer, I've recorded and edited countless hours of class video lectures. From this time spent editing, I've noticed every teacher has a transition word or phrase, and that these catch-phrases have something in common. Here are a few examples: "Making sense?" "Tracking with me?" "Ready to move on?" These all are verbal attempts at informal checks, taking the pulse of our students to see whether or not they comprehend what we have just explained.

But such informal checks rarely elicit genuine feedback. We read the room looking for nodding heads and move on. **But what if we really paused to get feedback?** Polls are an effective and fast way to do just that. Note the transition points in your instruction, and at these points, use a poll to test for comprehension. Not only does this give us valuable feedback about our students' understanding, but it also gives us a real-time report on the effectiveness of our instruction.

#3 Chat for Immediate Feedback

Chat is perfect for real-time feedback. While we are teaching, we can ask our students or a teaching assistant to note what is confusing, unclear, and new or surprising in the chat window. We've noted this practice earlier as a way to employ informal checks for student learning, but it's also an effective tool to evaluate our teaching practices in-the-moment. Similar to polling, this real-time reporting from our students can give us more timely and accurate information about what's work and what's not working. At the end of a teaching session, we can ask our learners an evaluative question such as, "What has helped or detracted from your ability to learn today?" When class ends, Zoom saves a text file of all your student chat responses, so you can review them before the next time you teach.

#4 Make Feedback a Process

To be responsive to feedback, we need a process. A colleague of mine and counseling educator creates what he calls a *Weekly Feedback Loop* in his course. It's a simple system, a survey on his course site where students can submit feedback and questions during or after each class meeting. But what makes it work is his process. Each week he reviews the responses and begins the next class by referencing the input from the previous week. The routine is straightforward and only takes 15-30 minutes to process. It includes 1) a place to leave feedback, 2) a regular time to review the feedback, and 3) a consistent way to respond to the feedback.

Educator Stephen Brookfield uses a method he calls a CIQ: Critical Incident Questionnaire.[4] The CIQ is a five-minute exercise where students reflect on their engagement, disengagement, and what the teacher or other students did during the class session that advanced or hindered their learning. His process is similar: "I review them before the first class meeting of the following week. I make a note of the dominant themes and begin the next class by sharing with the students a brief report." Brookfield's approach is learner-centered and meta-cognitive (reflecting on the process of learning). Another strength of the CIQ is it casts the learner—not the teacher—as the locus of learning, which reinforces student ownership and responsibility.

Both examples are from college or graduate settings where classes meet once a week. However, you may be in a context where your classes meet daily or several times a week. In that case, it will probably be more realistic to use a method like the CIQ on a weekly basis.

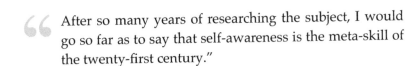

> After so many years of researching the subject, I would go so far as to say that self-awareness is the meta-skill of the twenty-first century."
>
> - Tasha Eurich, *Insight*

#5 Make it Automatic (as much as possible)

They say the best way to build a savings account is to set up automatic deposits. Automation works because it bypasses emotional resistance. We encounter psychological barriers to saving money, like the fear we won't have enough or might miss out on the chance to purchase something. Because of this, we put off saving. Similar emotions keep us from eliciting feedback: fear that we really are terrible at teaching, fear our students will become overly critical, a concern that we are creating unrealistic expectations, the need to get it right the first time, and the list goes on. I believe this emotional hurdle is why so very few educators ask for regular feedback. We need a means to bypass the resistance and make the feedback automatic. Here are a few ideas to help automate feedback:

- In your Learning Management System, create a feedback survey like the CIQ or *Weekly Feedback Loop*. Copy the survey and put an instance into each week, or another interval, within your course site. Send the link to students via the chat window in Zoom.
- If you share slide presentation files with your learners, place a link to a feedback survey on the last slide for every class.
- Create a reminder slide at the end of your presentations that directs students to the survey.

#6 Keep the Feedback Process Simple

A 5-question survey may overwhelm your learners, so consider using a single question. Here are a few examples:

- What would most improve your learning experience during the next class meeting?
- What worked or helped you learn most during this class session?
- The most important thing you should know about how I best learn is…
- After today's class session, what are you most curious about?

AFTERWORD

I began writing this book in the Summer of 2019, several months before the outbreak of COVID-19. When, in March of 2020, we found ourselves in a global pandemic, I was disappointed that the book was incomplete and that I had missed a crucial window when it might have benefited educators and students. However, friends and colleagues reminded me that teaching with Zoom was more than a response to a crisis. It's a form of teaching that will be with us for the long-term. So, I slowed down and reconnected with the goal of the book: to help educators teach thoughtfully and effectively in this video-mediated learning space.

I hope the book has helped readers who find themselves sent sideways by urgency and the unexpected. At the same time, I hope these chapters help you to slow down and consider long-term strategies and new practices to incorporate into your teaching.

Reader, on behalf of your students, I want to say "Thank you" for your hard work and the extra hours you're investing to adapt your material and teaching practices to this new learning environment. May you experience the fruits of your labor and those transformational moments that fuel our love for teaching.

NOTES

Introduction

1. Videoconferencing can be spelled as one word or two. In *Online Teaching with Zoom*, I've chosen to spell it as a single word.
2. See Cal Newport's two books, *Deep Work* and *Digital Minimalism*.
3. https://support.zoom.us/

1. The Equipment

1. https://excellentonlineteaching.com/otwz-chapter-1-resources/
2. Download the *Classroom Protocols template* at https://excellentonlineteaching.com/otwz-chapter-10-resources/

2. Prepare Your Classroom

1. https://support.zoom.us/hc/en-us/articles/205683899-Hot-Keys-and-Keyboard-Shortcuts-for-Zoom
2. https://support.zoom.us/hc/en-us/articles/209605493-In-meeting-file-transfer
3. https://excellentonlineteaching.com/otwz-chapter-2-resources/
4. https://zoom.us/test
5. https://excellentonlineteaching.com/otwz-chapter-2-resources/

3. Testing and Technical Difficulties

1. https://zoom.us/test
2. https://excellentonlineteaching.com/otwz-chapter-3-resources/
3. https://support.zoom.us/hc/en-us/articles/201362663-Joining-a-meeting-by-phone

4. Sharing

1. https://excellentonlineteaching.com/otwz-chapter-4-resources/
2. When I use the term, "plenary session," I am referring to the large group setting where every learner is on the screen. This is in contrast to the small group or breakout setting. "Plenary" will be used interchangeably with "large group."
3. This cannot be done with Apple Keynote in a single-monitor setup because Keynote only triggers *presenter view* if you have more than one monitor.

5. Breakout Room Basics

1. https://support.zoom.us/hc/en-us/articles/206476093-Enabling-breakout-rooms
2. https://support.zoom.us/hc/en-us/articles/206476313-Managing-breakout-rooms
3. https://support.zoom.us/hc/en-us/articles/360032752671-Pre-assigning-participants-to-breakout-rooms

7. Polls

1. Download the bonus material at https://excellentonlineteaching.com/otwz-bonus/

8. Security

1. https://excellentonlineteaching.com/otwz-chapter-8-resources/
2. https://support.zoom.us/hc/en-us/articles/201363333

9. The Student Perspective

1. The feedback gathered is based on my work with students in graduate and high school settings beginning in 2008 using Elluminate, Adobe Connect, Skype, and Zoom videoconferencing. They are not from a formal study but are thematic issues from conversations with students, course evaluations, surveys, and focus groups.
2. Download the bonus material at https://excellentonlineteaching.com/otwz-bonus/

10. Classroom Protocols

1. https://excellentonlineteaching.com/otwz-chapter-10-resources/
2. https://zoom.us/test
3. Olt, Phillip A. "Virtually There: Distant Freshmen Blended in Classes through Synchronous Online Education." *Innovative Higher Education* 43, no. 5 (October 2018): 381–95.

11. Key Instructional Practices

1. https://excellentonlineteaching.com/otwz-bonus/
2. https://excellentonlineteaching.com/otwz-chapter-11-resources/
3. See the previous chapter on *Classroom Protocols* for more information on how to prepare your students for this type of responsive environment.
4. Curt Thompson MD. "A Body of Work," April 15, 2020. https://curtthompsonmd.com/a-body-of-work/.
5. Brown, Peter C. *Make It Stick: The Science of Successful Learning*. Cambridge, Massachusetts: The Belknap Press of Harvard University Press, 2014, 67-101.
6. Deslauriers, Louis, Logan S. McCarty, Kelly Miller, Kristina Callaghan, and Greg Kestin. "Measuring Actual Learning versus Feeling of Learning in Response to

Being Actively Engaged in the Classroom." *Proceedings of the National Academy of Sciences* 116, no. 39 (September 24, 2019): 19251–57.

7. Ibid.
8. See setup details at https://support.zoom.us/hc/en-us/articles/209605493-In-meeting-file-transfer

12. 30 Active Learning Methods

1. That's a critical statement and one that should be supported. Because we are not able to do a deep dive into education theories and the research on active learning, I'll supply references at the *Online Teaching with Zoom* webpage for this this chapter. https://excellentonlineteaching.com/otwz-chapter-12-resources/
2. MacIsaac, Dan, ed. *"Twilight of the Lecture by Craig Lambert* , Harvard Magazine. *The Physics Teacher* 51, no. 4 (April 2013): 254–254.
3. https://excellentonlineteaching.com/otwz-bonus
4. https://jigsaw.org

14. Establishing Groups

1. https://excellentonlineteaching.com/otwz-chapter-14-resources/
2. Patrick Lencioni's works are perhaps the most helpful resources for developing a better understanding of team cohesion. See his books, *The 5 Dysfunctions of a Team* and *The Advantage.*
3. Scott, Kim. *Radical Candor How to Get What You Want by Saying What You Mean.* London: Pan Books, 2019.
4. Brookfield, Stephen, and Stephen Preskill. *The Discussion Book: 50 Great Ways to Get People Talking.* First edition. San Francisco, CA: John Wiley & Sons, 2016, 233.

15. Group Etiquette

1. https://excellentonlineteaching.com/otwz-chapter-15-resources/

16. Breakout Sizes and Dynamics

1. At the time of this writing, depending on your license, Zoom can accommodate up to 10,000 participants in a webinar and up to 500 in a meeting.

18. Discussion Guides

1. https://excellentonlineteaching.com/otwz-chapter-18-resources/

19. Facilitating Breakouts

1. For more on this, see my post at https://excellentonlineteaching.com/3-reasons-why-videoconference-classrooms-feel-awkward/
2. Brookfield, Stephen, and Stephen Preskill. *Discussion as a Way of Teaching: Tools and Techniques for Democratic Classrooms.* 2nd ed. San Francisco: Jossey-Bass, 2005, 64-65.
3. Tanner, Kimberly D. "Structure Matters: Twenty-One Teaching Strategies to Promote Student Engagement and Cultivate Classroom Equity." *CBE—Life Sciences Education* 12, no. 3 (September 2013): 322–31
4. Pranikoff, Kara. *Teaching Talk: A Practical Guide to Fostering Student Thinking and Conversation.* Portsmouth, NH: Heinemann, 2017, 103.
5. Psychologist, Lev Vygotsky developed this term, often shorted to ZPD. He defines this as "the distance between the actual developmental level as determined by independent problem solving and the level of potential development as determined through problem-solving under adult guidance, or in collaboration with more capable peers"

    Vygotskij, Lev Semenovič, and Michael Cole. *Mind in Society: The Development of Higher Psychological Processes.* Nachdr. Cambridge, Mass.: Harvard Univ. Press, 1981, 86.
6. Bungay Stanier, Michael. *The Coaching Habit: Say Less, Ask More & Change the Way You Lead Forever.* Toronto: Box of Crayons Press, 2016, 39.
7. https://excellentonlineteaching.com/otwz-chapter-19-resources/
8. Brookfield, Stephen, and Stephen Preskill. *Discussion as a Way of Teaching: Tools and Techniques for Democratic Classrooms.* 2nd ed. San Francisco: Jossey-Bass, 2005, 90.

20. Improving Our Game

1. Schein, Edgar H., and Peter A. Schein. *Humble Leadership: The Power of Relationships, Openness, and Trust.* First edition. Oakland, CA: Berrett-Koehler Publishers, Inc, 2018.
2. https://visible-learning.org/hattie-ranking-influences-effect-sizes-learning-achievement/
3. https://excellentonlineteaching.com/otwz-chapter-20-resources/
4. You can download a word document copy of Brookfields CIQ instrument at http://www.stephenbrookfield.com/critical-incident-questionnaire

ACKNOWLEDGMENTS

To my wife, Jenah: I'm grateful for your support and encouragement during this year of writing. This project would not have been possible without your wisdom and belief.

I want to express my gratitude to the many teachers and instructional designers who provided feedback and recommended edits to early drafts of text: Marie Beamer, David Brown, Chris Dickerson, Darryl Meekins, Kathleen Korondi, Darryl Meekins, Michael Morrison, Stephaney Morrison, Kathy Perez, Christine Roseveare, and Jeff Weiberg.

To Barbara Oakley: Your feedback transformed this text and has helped me grow as a writer.

To Josh Bleeker, Joshua Cast, Will Haugerude, Torrence Jackson, Tim Koller, Matt Toth, and Shawn Trueman: Your words of guidance and encouragement came at critical moments. Thank you.

To the Faculty at Denver Seminary: Thank you for the many hours you've invested with me learning how to teach thoughtfully in this new learning space. This book is, in so many ways, the result of our work together.

ABOUT THE AUTHOR

Aaron Johnson is an Associate Dean of Educational Technology at Denver Seminary in Littleton, Colorado. He has spent fifteen years in the field of online education, as a high school teacher, instructional designer, and faculty developer. His book *Excellent Online Teaching: Effective Strategies for a Successful Semester Online* has been an Amazon Bestseller, and used by hundreds of K-12 through Graduate programs throughout the world. His undergraduate work in video production and media studies, helps him to think critically about the tendencies of technologies and how to thoughtfully use them to support student learning. His graduate work explored how students experience personal and social transformation in the online learning environment. The question, "How are people formed through learning experiences?" continues to drive his work.

Mr. Johnson has consulted and led workshop trainings for state university systems, international schools, and online school districts. This work is motivated by his desire to simplify the work of distance educators by helping them focus on the key practices that most benefit student learning.

An avid hiker, Johnson has explored hundreds of miles of Colorado's Front Range and wilderness areas. His hiking website, Dayhikes Near Denver, is used by over one million people each year.

He lives with his wife and two daughters in Castle Rock, Colorado.

To contact Aaron Johnson: aaron@excellentonlineteaching.com

Or visit: https://excellentonlineteaching.com

ALSO BY THE AUTHOR
EXCELLENT ONLINE TEACHING

Book 1 in the Excellent Online Teaching Series

Purchase *Excellent Online Teaching: Effective Strategies for a Successful Semester Online* today at Amazon.com

https://excellentonlineteaching.com

If you have enjoyed this book, I'd be grateful for your review on Amazon.

Made in the USA
Middletown, DE
06 January 2021